Facebook® in O[ne] F[...]

DENNIS KENNEDY AND ALLISON C. SHIELDS

ABA LawPracticeManagementSection

MARKETING · MANAGEMENT · TECHNOLOGY · FINANCE

15 14 13 12   5 4 3 2 1

Library of Congress Cataloging-in-Publication Data

Kennedy, Dennis M., 1958–
    Facebook in one hour for lawyers / Dennis Kennedy and Allison C. Shields.
      p. cm.
    Includes index.
    ISBN 978-1-61438-543-1
  1. Facebook (Electronic resource) 2. Internet in legal services—United States. 3. Online social networks—United States. 4. Social media—United States. 5. Lawyers—United States—Handbooks, manuals, etc. I. Shields, Allison (Allison C.), 1969– II. American Bar Association. Section of Law Practice Management. III. Title.
    KF320.I57.K46   2012
    006.7'54—dc23

2012023260

Table of Contents

About the Authors

 **Dennis Kennedy** is an information technology lawyer, as well as a widely published author and frequent speaker on legal technology and Internet topics. He writes the technology column for the *ABA Journal*, co-wrote with Allison Shields the book, *LinkedIn in One Hour for Lawyers*, co-wrote with Tom Mighell the book, *The Lawyer's Guide to Collaboration Tools and Technologies: Smart Ways to Work Together*, and co-hosts the highly regarded legal technology podcast, *The Kennedy-Mighell Report*, on the Legal Talk Network. His blog, *DennisKennedy.Blog* (**http://denniskennedy.com/blog/**), is a respected resource on legal technology topics. Photo by Dan Donovan.

 **Allison C. Shields** is the author of the *Legal Ease Blog* (**www.legaleaseconsulting.com**) and President of Legal Ease Consulting, Inc., where she coaches lawyers on practice management and business development issues, including how to use social networking effectively as a marketing tool. She is a former practicing lawyer, law firm manager, and administrative partner. A nationally recognized speaker, Ms. Shields presents workshops and programs in both private and public settings. She is also the author of numerous articles on practice management and business development/marketing issues. Ms. Shields's website, *Lawyer Meltdown* (**www.LawyerMeltdown.com**), provides resources and information for lawyers about managing and building their practices. She is the co-author, with Dennis Kennedy, of *LinkedIn in One Hour for Lawyers*.

Acknowledgments

Thanks to Denise Constantine and the great team on the LPM Publishing staff for turning our draft into the finished book you are reading; to the Law Practice Management Section Publishing Board for letting us write on this important topic; to Jennifer Ator, Tom Mighell, and Carole Levitt for their very helpful, detailed comments on the first draft of this book; to Evelyn Kennedy for always wanting her son to write books; to Grace Kennedy for proofreading and other editing assistance; to our Facebook and real-world friends, who remind us every day of the value of friendships; and to our families, for their tireless patience, understanding, and support during the process of creating this book, and the rest of the time as well.

Introduction
The Facebook Phenomenon and
Why Lawyers Are Using Facebook

Although we have proven to ourselves that it is actually possible to read the Lessons section of this book in one hour, that's not the best way to read this book. You will want to spend more time than that because this book is chock-full of instructions, practical suggestions, tips, and ideas about how lawyers and legal professionals can use Facebook.

You might read the book in one sitting to get a good overview of Facebook, its features, and the ways you might use it. Or you might read it one Lesson at a time and then go to Facebook and implement what you learned. You could use it as a reference guide that you return to as you use Facebook and have questions, even keeping it by your computer. Law firms might use it as a training manual. We think of this book as both a guide and companion for Facebook users.

Facebook is a bona fide Internet phenomenon with sometimes surprising real-world implications. Starting in 2003 as a simple online version of a college picture book for classmates, Facebook has grown exponentially into the premier platform people of all kinds use to connect and communicate. It is the best example of what social media and social networking are and how they work. Facebook is a tool that helps you make your networks—in the real world and online—more visible and usable than they are when they are only in your head. You can map your networks, organize them, grow and nurture them, and efficiently use them both for your own benefit and for the benefit of your friends.

At the time this book was written, Facebook had completed an IPO and had more than 900 million members, an astonishing percentage of whom use the platform on a daily basis for a significant period of time. If Facebook were a nation, it would be the third most-populated country on the planet. It is a new, uncharted, and expansive territory, with much still be explored and fewer certainties than most of us would like.

Facebook users often see Facebook in different ways because their experience emphasizes different aspects. For example, Dennis appreciates Facebook as another channel for his writing and the home for his high school reunion group, while Allison has always focused on the Page element of Facebook for her business. Some see Facebook as a great games platform, a way to talk with friends on a daily basis, a photo-sharing service, and much more. The versatility of Facebook confuses lawyers when they hear that Facebook is the place they "must" be for legal marketing, especially when they compare Facebook to LinkedIn, the social networking service that most lawyers use.

As we've spoken to lawyers about social media over the past few years, the most notable change we've seen when we poll our audiences is the greatly increased number of lawyers who say that they are now using Facebook. While LinkedIn probably still remains the most popular social networking platform for lawyers, its large lead over Facebook has diminished greatly over the last year or so. Although we will discuss the personal versus professional divide in more detail in the Advanced Topics section, lawyers do seem to be using Facebook for personal networking and LinkedIn for professional networking, although there is often significant overlap.

In spite of this trend, lawyers tell us that they simply don't understand Facebook, don't see the value for lawyers, and want us to tell them exactly how lawyers can benefit from Facebook.

As lawyers should well know by now, it depends. As a group, lawyers are smart and perceptive. If they understand a topic, they know how to spot issues, identify opportunities, and balance risks. Our approach when speaking to lawyers about Facebook is to help them understand how Facebook works, what its features are, and how they can make use of it. Invariably, lawyers will come up with plenty of ideas about how they might use Facebook after they learn the basics. Or they may decide that Facebook makes sense for them to use for a personal presence, but not a professional presence.

This book emphasizes the *how-to* more so than the *why* of Facebook for lawyers, even though you will find quite a bit of the *why* sprinkled throughout this book.

Why Should Lawyers Use Facebook?

As we were writing this book and speaking about Facebook for lawyers, this was the question we heard most often, so we'll try to answer it here. But as social media use (and Facebook itself) evolves, the answer is likely to change.

Right now, many lawyers are using Facebook on a personal level, but they're not sure how to use it for business. Some scoff at the mere suggestion that Facebook can be used at all in the practice of law, for business development, or otherwise. But at its core, all social networking, whether online or in the real world, is most effective when it is used to communicate and build relationships. If the people you want to reach or with whom you want to build relationships are using that particular platform on a consistent basis, as is increasingly the case with Facebook, it might be wise to explore ways to use that platform to help you meet those people and allow them to get to know you, both as a professional and as a person. In other words, you need to go to where your target audience is.

We are about to reach an era where young lawyers entering the profession will have spent most of their Internet lives on Facebook, and older lawyers will have been pushed into Facebook to see pictures of their grandchildren and to communicate with their children. No one knows what the Facebook era will look like, but it does not seem realistic to say that you can simply avoid it.

What Can Lawyers Do to Benefit Professionally from Facebook?

The other question we often hear, in one form or another, is, "How can lawyers benefit from Facebook?" The real question is often, "What do I do so Facebook brings me new business and new clients?" Lawyers wonder why what they've done with websites, blogs, LinkedIn, Twitter, advertising, and more is not enough. They worry that Facebook is just the latest fad, and they seem to enjoy telling us that they haven't obtained new clients from Facebook, as if that demonstrates something about Facebook rather than their use of it.

For websites, blogs, LinkedIn, and the like, you can find hundreds of articles purporting to tell lawyers exactly what five or ten steps they must take to have success and bring in business. Experts seem to be everywhere. With Facebook, you don't see as many "experts" and the five-step guides don't seem to exist. In part, that's because Facebook is evolving; it's relatively new, large, and somewhat uncharted territory. However, it's also because Facebook maps to real-world relationships, so each person's use of Facebook is individualized. While writing this book we found it striking how much our everyday use of Facebook differed. The friends you have and how they use Facebook will also have an impact on your use of Facebook.

Given the somewhat personalized way each of us uses Facebook, we nonetheless wanted to get your thinking started by giving you a list of ways that lawyers might benefit from using Facebook.

- Create a supplement to your formal website with a Page for your firm that's more informal and informative enough that people will "Like" the Page (Lesson 4).
- Use the Timeline to tell a compelling story about the history of your firm or your career, emphasizing highlights (Lesson 3).
- Post informative Updates about issues and developments in your practice area so that Friends remember that you work in that area and make referrals to you (Lesson 7).
- Use Facebook Events to publicize and manage presentations for clients and others (Lesson 10).
- Participate in Groups related to your practice area to make connections with others in the field (Lesson 8).
- Create your own Group to publicize a practice area, reach a target market, or create an interactive version of your firm newsletter (Lesson 8).
- Comment on, Like, or Share others' links or Share Updates of your own to engage in conversations and interact with influencers and potential referrers (Lesson 7).
- Quickly and easily monitor what is happening in your network (Lesson 9).
- Use the personal elements of Facebook to put a human face on your professional presence (Lesson 3).

People do business with people they know, like, and trust. If you use Facebook with that in mind, and with a goal of getting to know others, Facebook might well be a good way to develop business.

However, most lawyers will say that they joined Facebook or were asked to join Facebook by a friend or family member. Part of the message of this book is that using Facebook for personal reasons can be highly valuable and rewarding. Dennis often describes his high school reunion Facebook group as the best benefit of being on Facebook. You can read this book and get plenty of help for using Facebook effectively for personal reasons, and we think it is okay if you want to use Facebook for just these purposes.

There are three essential parts of your Facebook presence that you need to understand well: Identity (Profile/Timeline), Friends, and Participation. Understand these three building blocks and you'll go a long way toward "getting" Facebook and will most likely find the time spent on Facebook valuable.

- **Identity** on Facebook allows you to establish a Profile explaining who you are and a Timeline that shows people things about you that happen over time. These components, and especially the photos you use with them, give people a good sense of who you are.
- **Friends** are the people you are connected to in your networks. Facebook lets you identify people in your existing networks (e.g., your Outlook contacts) who have Facebook accounts and find new people. You can invite them all to connect to you by sending them a Friend request ("Friending"). By accepting Friend requests, people show that they are connected to each other and, in some cases, such as family relationships, can show the nature of those connections.
- **Participation** is cultivating, tending, and engaging with your Facebook network. If you are not finding value in Facebook, it's most likely because you have neglected this key aspect of Facebook. Social media is participatory media. You need to put effort into your online networking just as you do in your real-world networks.

This book is organized into two major sections: Lessons and Advanced Topics. In Lessons, we cover key subjects to get you quickly up to speed on Facebook, whether you are a complete beginner or a longtime user. This section is the core of the book. In Advanced Topics, we cover some important issues (such as legal ethics) and advanced features and resources to help you enrich your Facebook experience and make better use of its tools.

Our Agenda

- **Lesson 1. Getting Started—Setting Up Your Facebook Account and a Quick Orientation.** We cover the basics of opening or revitalizing your account and give you a quick orientation to Facebook navigation and search tools.

- **Lesson 2. Optimizing Your Privacy and Other Settings.** Privacy issues in Facebook have long been a subject for discussion and concern. These settings are so important that we address them up front to give you a good understanding of the implications of the settings and to get you off to a good start so Facebook works for you and not against you.

- **Lesson 3. Creating Your Profile and Managing Your Timeline.** Your Identity is established through your Profile and through the relatively new Timeline. We discuss ways to set up your Profile to present yourself in the best light and then manage your Timeline to your best advantage.

- **Lesson 4. Establishing a Page for Your Firm or Practice.** Although Facebook historically has focused on individual users, the focus on opportunities for businesses has increased. Pages, as opposed to Profiles, are what you use to create a law firm or practice page. We show you ways you might benefit from Pages and how you can use them.

- **Lesson 5. Friending Effectively.** The second Facebook essential is Friends—the connections in your network. We get you started with the idea of Friending and show you good ways to invite people to become your Friends and accept Friend invitations. We also discuss ways to grow and evolve your network of Friends.

■ **Lesson 6. Organizing with Friend Lists.** Facebook offers several ways to organize and manage Friends so you can control the information they receive or can see. One of the easiest tools to use, but not widely known, is Friend Lists. We walk you through these tools and how they improve your Facebook experience.

■ **Lesson 7. Participating by Updates, Comments, Likes, and Sharing.** Participation is the third essential component of using Facebook. We cover the most commonly used and simplest tools for participating in Facebook.

■ **Lesson 8. Participation Through Messages, Groups, and Subscriptions.** Facebook gives you many ways to connect and communicate with your Friends. We discuss some of the more interactive participation tools here.

■ **Lesson 9. Monitoring Your Facebook Network.** You need to pay attention to and cultivate your networks. We introduce you to ways to monitor your Facebook network, including your Home Page, Timeline, e-mail notifications, and the official Facebook mobile app.

■ **Lesson 10. Other Features You Should Know.** Facebook is a rich and complex platform. Features that work best for one person might not interest another. In this Lesson, we sample the variety of Facebook's options and point out features that might benefit you.

■ **Conclusion: Developing a Strategic Approach and Three Easy Steps.** We conclude the Lessons section with some ideas to help you develop a basic Facebook strategy that works for you. We end with three action steps you can take right away to increase Facebook's benefit to you.

- **Advanced Topics.** In this section, we give you a quick overview of some advanced topics, issues especially of interest to lawyers, and ways to improve your use of Facebook, including:
  - ▶ ethical considerations
  - ▶ separating your personal from your professional presence
  - ▶ Facebook apps
  - ▶ litigation and discovery issues
  - ▶ tips
  - ▶ helpful resources

Facebook is an incredibly popular social media platform. Given the number of people using Facebook, it's inevitable that lawyers will join the world of Facebook. The big question is how will Facebook work for you? Will it be a personal tool or a practice tool? If you are going to be on the platform—and it's difficult to imagine how you will stay away from it—it only makes sense to use it in ways that are comfortable, appropriate, and tailored to you. That's what this book will help you do.

Glossary

As we were writing this book, we realized that people use different terms to refer to the same thing when they talk about Facebook, and sometimes they use terms that are different from those Facebook uses. Perhaps the best example is that many individuals refer to their "Facebook pages" while Facebook uses the term *Page* to refer to the Facebook presence created by a business and *Profile* for that of an individual. Interestingly, it's becoming more common to hear people simply refer to their individual Facebook presence as just "their Facebook." As a result, we begin with a glossary of terms and the way we use them in this book.

Business Account. An account that is created solely to administer a Page or Facebook Ads. Business Accounts have limited functionality, as described more fully in Lesson 4.

Friending. The bilateral process of inviting people to be Friends and accepting Friend invitations (Lesson 5).

Friends. Your connections on Facebook and the components of your network; also, people who have accepted Friend invitations from you or from whom you have accepted Friend invitations (Lesson 5).

Home Page. The page to which Facebook directs you when you click on the **Home** link at the top of the blue navigation bar anywhere in Facebook; a "dashboard" page where your News Feed and other commonly used tools are located (Lesson 1 and Lesson 9).

News Feed. A running list of stories (also called Updates or posts), pictures, comments, and more from your Friends, people to whom you Subscribe, and Pages you have Liked. It's located in the center column of your Home Page (Lesson 1 and Lesson 9).

Page. The Facebook presence of a business. Compare to *Profile*, the term used for the Facebook presence of an individual (Lesson 4).

Post. Either the act of uploading any content to Facebook or a collective term to cover types of content uploaded to Facebook, including Updates, photos, comments, and so on. People commonly use the term *post* interchangeably with *Update*.

Profile. The information you, as an individual, provide to Facebook about yourself. It includes the About section, which has work and education information, as well as information about your Likes, interests, music, and other data you choose to share. The term *Profile* is for the Facebook presence of an individual, and the term *Page* is for the Facebook presence of a business (Lesson 3).

Timeline. The place where you share content with others on Facebook. In the old Facebook format, it used to be called the Wall. You can reach your Timeline by clicking your name or photo in the blue navigation bar at the top of any page in Facebook (Lesson 3).

Wall. The area of Facebook where you used to post Updates or shared content; your Friends could also post on your Wall. The Wall has been replaced with the Timeline (Lesson 3).

A Note on Changes in Facebook. Facebook's layout, format, and naming conventions seem to change frequently. As an example, if we had written this book in 2011, we would have had a lot of coverage of the Wall. Now, the Wall has all but disappeared from this book because the Timeline has replaced it. Please keep this in mind as you read this book. Even if step-by-step instructions or screenshots become outdated or inaccurate, the concepts should remain similar, and you should be able to figure out how to accomplish the same tasks. Understanding basic navigation concepts, such as how hovering your mouse pointer in certain locations brings up a contextual menu like right-clicking a mouse does in most computer programs, will also help you keep current. The Resources section of this book includes a number of resources that should continue to provide useful information about changes. Finally, check out the Social Networking for Lawyers Group we've created in Facebook, where we'll try to provide updates to this book.

Getting Started
Setting Up Your Facebook Account and a Quick Orientation

In this Lesson, we will first help you create or reactivate your Facebook account. The process is simple and familiar for anyone who has ever set up any online account for e-mail or any other web-based service. We also cover some very basic elements of Facebook navigation to help beginners get an orientation to Facebook and some of its main features. This discussion will also be a useful review for anyone who does not use Facebook on a regular basis.

Even though more than 900 million people have already joined Facebook, many new users join Facebook every day. Don't worry—it's not too late for you to get started. In fact, even if you are a complete beginner, by the time you finish this book you can be among the best users of Facebook in the legal community.

Let's start at the most basic level. Facebook is an online service you use on the Internet, not a software program you install. Facebook is a good example of what people today call "cloud computing." You do not have to have a certain type of computer to use Facebook—any computer, tablet device, or smartphone connected to the Internet will do the job. You open your account and use Facebook by visiting the Facebook website using your Internet browser (Internet Explorer, Firefox, Chrome, Safari—it doesn't matter which). You can then use Facebook anytime and anywhere you have Internet access—at home or work or on a mobile device.

Confirming or Setting Up Your Account

Do you have a working Facebook account? Readers of this book will fall into three categories:

1. If you already have a Facebook account, know your password, and can log into your account, skip directly to the **A Quick Orientation to Facebook** section below or move on to Lesson 2.

2. If you already have a Facebook account, but haven't used it for a while and no longer know your password and cannot log into your account, you will need to reset your password and confirm that you can log into your account. Go to the Facebook website (**www.facebook.com**) and attempt to log into your account using the e-mail address you used when you set up the account. If this fails, have the password reset by clicking on the **Forgot Password?** link. Facebook will send you an e-mail with a new temporary password. Use the link in this e-mail to log into your account and then create a new password that you will vow to remember or store securely. Once you can log into your account, skip to the **A Quick Orientation to Facebook** section below or go on to Lesson 2.

3. If you do not have a Facebook account or can no longer access an account you created, you will need to register a new account. Setting up a new account is similar to setting up an account with any other web service. Go to the Facebook website and complete the Sign Up form (see Figure 1.1).

When creating a Facebook account using this screen, you must use your real name, not a fake name or pseudonym. You cannot use a business name to sign up for this type of account. To set up an account solely for business use, with no personal Profile attached, see Lesson 4.

Figure 1.1: Sign Up Page

Facebook requires you to verify your account by replying to a confirming e-mail. As part of the sign-up process, you must provide a valid and working personal e-mail address. Facebook does not allow you to create a personal account using an addresss like **info@ yourlawfirm.com**. We recommend using an e-mail account that you expect to have for a long time, like a Gmail, Hotmail, or other web-based e-mail account. You will be asked to re-enter your e-mail address to make sure it is correct.

You will also need to create a password. Facebook accounts are notorious for being hacked, so it's essential to use a strong password—a combination of upper- and lowercase letters, numbers, and symbols. Security experts currently recommend that you use at least twelve characters in your password. You definitely want to avoid using common or easy-to-guess passwords ("password1" or "qwerty"). Remember to use a different password for Facebook than you use for any other account.

Finally, you must provide your gender and birthdate. Birthday greetings are a big tradition on Facebook because Facebook notifies you about your Friends' birthdays. In Lesson 2, we talk about how you can later control whether you allow people to see your gender and birthday information.

Once you complete the form, click on the **Sign Up** button. You'll be taken to a screen that requires you to type in a set of random characters ("captcha") to confirm that you are a human rather than an automated script. Type in those characters and click **Sign Up**.

Note that by clicking on Sign Up, you are agreeing to Facebook's Statement of Rights and Responsibilities and Privacy Policy. We recommend that you take the time to read these documents to understand how Facebook will use your data, especially if you are a lawyer. Facebook collects its privacy policies at **www.facebook.com/about/privacy/**. You can learn about what data is collected and why, how changes to the policies are made, and much more.

When you get the confirming e-mail from Facebook (probably in a matter of seconds), click on the link provided and log into your new Facebook account.

Getting Started Wizard for New Users

Facebook orients new users with a quick, three-step Getting Started Wizard. We'll go into detail about the three components of the wizard later, but for now the Getting Started Wizard will help you get off to a quick start.

First, you can import contacts from your Gmail or other e-mail service and identify contacts who are members of Facebook. You can then easily invite some of these contacts to be your Friends. Although this step might seem appealing, we suggest that you take it slow and read Lesson 5 (and maybe Separating Your Personal from Your Professional Presence in Advanced Topics) before you start to add Friends.

Second, you can set up your basic Profile. At this point, Facebook asks for only a small amount of biographical and personal information. Lawyers familiar with LinkedIn might be surprised at how little biographical or résumé information is in the Facebook Profile. (We discuss Profiles in more detail in Lesson 3.) The focus here is to add information about your high school, college or university, and employer. This information helps people find you on Facebook and identify you as the person for whom they're looking.

Third, you can add your Profile picture. (We'll also talk about Profile pictures in Lesson 3.) We cannot overstate how important pictures are in the Facebook world. Choose an appropriate digital photo on your computer and upload it to your Facebook account.

After you finish the Getting Started Wizard, you will arrive at your Home page. On this first visit to your Home page, you will see a welcome message with some suggestions about what to do next. These include editing your Profile, activating Facebook on your mobile phone, and searching for Friends. As you begin using Facebook, the Home page will change, and the welcome information and suggestions will be replaced by your News Feed.

A Quick Orientation to Facebook

Your Facebook experience will center around your Home page, so that's where we will start (see Figure 1.2). The Home page has five basic sections: a blue navigation menu bar at the top, three columns of information (the body of the Home page), and a footer menu.

The left column in the body of the Home page provides handy links to commonly used features. Think of it as a list of favorites or bookmarks as in your Internet browser. The middle column displays your News Feed of posts from your Friends. The right column shows upcoming events, suggestions about people to add as Friends, ads, and more.

Figure 1.2: Home Page

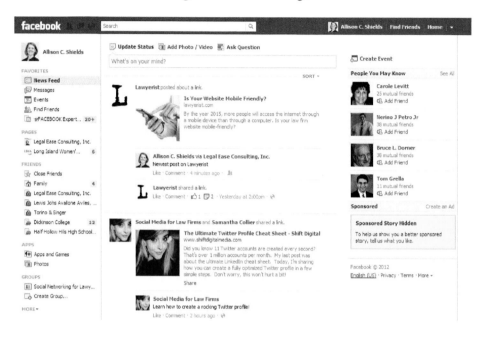

The footer provides links to Help, Privacy Policy, Terms, Creating a Page, and other administrative material.

Facebook Navigation Bar

The top blue navigation bar will stay the same regardless of where you are in Facebook (see Figure 1.3).

Figure 1.3: Facebook Navigation Bar

Clicking on the Facebook logo at the far left brings you to your Home page. The next icon, which looks like people, is the Friends icon. To the right is the Messages icon, and the last icon, which looks like a globe, is for Notifications. Clicking on these icons gives you options relating to Friends, Messages, and Notifications. A red bubble with a number appears on top of these icons as a signal of new activity related to that feature—new Friend requests, new Messages, or other Notifications, for example that Friends Liked or Commented on an Update or photo you posted.

Next to those icons on the navigation bar is the Facebook search feature. You can use the search bar to search for People, Groups, or Pages (as well as music and other interests) by typing a search term into the search bar. Figure 1.4 shows a search for "law practice management."

Figure 1.4: Facebook Search

If you're having trouble finding what you're looking for or if you want more results, click on **See more results for . . .** at the bottom of the search results box to see a full results page. To narrow your results, use the filters on the left side of the screen.

Back in the navigation bar, to the right of the search box, you'll see a thumbnail of your Profile picture and your name. Clicking on them will bring you to your Timeline. To the right, if you are new to Facebook, is the **Find Friends** link, which we'll talk more about in Lesson 5. When you have been on Facebook for a time, this link will disappear. To the right of that is the **Home** link, which brings you to your Home page. And finally, you'll see the **downward facing triangle**. Any time you see that triangle on Facebook, it indicates that there are additional options. In the navigation bar, clicking on this triangle reveals options including your account and privacy settings (which we discuss in Lesson 2) and the Help link.

Left Column—Home Page Navigation

The main navigation for your Facebook activities is on your Home page along the left side of the screen (see Figure 1.5). The "bookmarks" on the left of your Home page are for navigating easily to other areas to view your Messages, Events, Photos, Pages, Friend Lists, etc. You can customize your experience by adding frequently used locations to your bookmarked Favorites. To edit any of the bookmarks in the navigation bar, hover your mouse over it until you see the pencil icon appear and click on the "Add to favorites" menu item.

Favorites

By default, Favorites contains your **News Feed**, **Messages** (private messages and conversations with others on Facebook), **Events**, and **Find**

Figure 1.5: Home Page Navigation

Friends. We cover Friends in depth in Lesson 5, and we'll touch on Events in Lesson 10.

Apps

Next is a section of Apps. The first bookmark is **Photos**, which shows you Friends' photo posts and allows you to upload or access your own photos, videos, or albums.

Apps and Games takes you to a page where you can view featured Facebook apps or play games on Facebook.

Music helps you discover music you might like by showing you what your Friends are listening to. You can also look at Top Songs, Trending Albums, or Featured Music Services.

Pages

If you are the Administrator of a Page (discussed in Lesson 4), your Home bookmarks include links to those Pages and a small number next to the Page to show whether there has been activity or interaction on each Page.

Friends

Friends is the next section. It includes your Friend lists, some of which Facebook calls "Smart Lists." We discuss Friends in Lesson 6.

Groups

Next, Facebook displays the Groups you belong to, and offers a **Create a Group** link. We'll talk more about Groups in Lesson 8.

Interests

Clicking on the **MORE** link at the bottom of the list brings up Interests, which for Allison includes Interest Lists and Subscriptions, discussed in Advanced Topics and Lesson 7, respectively.

The News Feed

The center column of your Home page is your News Feed. The News Feed contains the Updates from your Friends and any Pages you have Liked. But you won't necessarily see everything your Friends post in your News Feed, or everything your "Liked" Pages post. To learn more about managing your News Feed, see Lesson 9.

Ticker

The Facebook Ticker appears to the right of the main News Feed, and it shows Facebook activity in real time. Just as people can only see posts, comments, and other Facebook activity on your Timeline, their Ticker shows only information you share with them.

If you're new to Facebook, you won't see Ticker on your Home page right away. Facebook has determined that Ticker is only useful to Facebook users with a certain level of activity on their Facebook account.

As a way of getting acquainted with Facebook, you might also take a quick stroll through the Help Center, which you access through **Help** in the footer (see Figure 1.6). This page is well organized and has links to common questions, especially questions beginners often have.

As you might have noticed in Figure 1.1, Facebook says that your account will always be free. As of the time this book is written, Facebook does not offer premium accounts, so you don't have to make a decision about whether to upgrade from the free account.

You should now have your account set up, be familiar with the Home page, and have a sense of some of the major Facebook features. Let's now move to Lesson 2, where we address important settings, including those for privacy.

Figure 1.6: Help Page

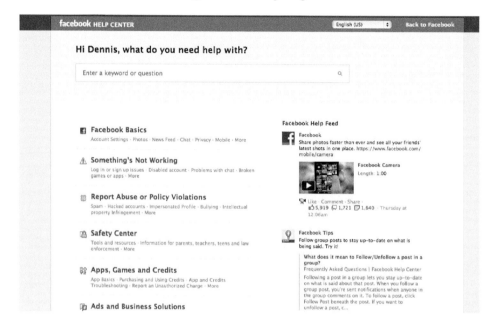

Optimizing Your Privacy and Other Settings

We think that Facebook privacy settings are so important that we are addressing them immediately. Even before we walk you through basic Facebook features, we want to emphasize how crucial it is that you pay attention to these settings.

Even if you know very little about Facebook or have never used it, you no doubt have heard or read alarming or controversial stories about privacy and the amount and types of personal information that Facebook has about its users. Lawyers often point to privacy as their main reservation about joining Facebook. As we mentioned in Lesson 1, lawyers should become familiar with Facebook's privacy policies (**www.facebook.com/about/privacy/**).

We cannot overestimate the importance of choosing appropriate privacy and other account settings on Facebook and any other social media platform. You must understand the implications of the settings to which you default or choose for yourself. As a general rule, default settings are best for the company offering the social media platform, not what might be best for you. Using data that users provide is an essential element in most monetization efforts by social media platforms.

The good news is that Facebook has worked over the years to give users much more control over privacy than ever before. Facebook has had a tendency to change its approach to privacy and settings more frequently than most of us like, but the changes have largely been positive responses to specific concerns users have raised. Facebook also gives you lots of ways to manage your privacy and audience, including a granular approach to customizing the audience for your content and other aspects of your Facebook presence. Facebook has also made it easier over time to find these controls and to change them.

We recommend systematically working your way through all the settings step by step, either when you create your account or the next time you use your account. It will take only a few minutes. Then plan to revisit your settings once or twice a year. You also need to review your settings if you learn that Facebook has made changes to privacy settings (Facebook changes tend to get a lot of coverage in the press and blogs) or if you notice that people whom you wouldn't expect have access to your information. Often a privacy concern can be remedied with a quick change to your settings.

General Principles

Facebook founder Mark Zuckerberg has indicated at various times that we should all want to share information about ourselves, that there is a great benefit to doing so, and that what we do on the Internet should be tied to our real-world identities. Keeping these basic premises in mind will help you greatly in determining the approach you want to take with Facebook.

Here are some key principles to keep in mind when setting up a Facebook account:

- **Assume Facebook wants you to share your information more than you do.** As a general rule, it's better for Facebook's business model if you share more of your data. Be wary of default settings, and consider it your responsibility to dial back privacy settings to match your level of comfort.

- **Assume that more people can see your Facebook activities than you think and act accordingly.** Even when you think that you have a good understanding of Facebook privacy and audience settings, you'll probably be surprised that more people than you expect can see what you've posted or what your Friends have posted about you. Behave as if what you put on Facebook might not just be in a newspaper, but as if your parents, children, grandparents, or grandchildren might see it. In fact, it's not a bad idea to assume that the person you'd least like to see your posting will, in fact, see it. The name of the game is good judgment.

- **There are excellent granular controls to fine-tune your privacy and audience.** You will see that many of the general concerns people have about using Facebook can be addressed through using settings thoughtfully. In fact, some of Facebook's settings even allow you to go back and clean up or hide items you posted in the past that you now see as potentially embarrassing.

- **Handling Facebook settings does NOT mean "set and forget."** Facebook often changes its approach or adds or reorganizes settings tools. Your approach or your needs might also change from time to time. Settings are something you must revisit on a regular basis.

Account Settings

Settings are easy to find. Look at the right-hand side of the blue Facebook navigation bar at the top of each page next to the Home button and you'll see a **small inverted triangle.** Click on it to access Account Settings and Privacy Settings (see Figure 2.1).

Figure 2.1: Home Submenu

Click on **Account Settings** and you'll see the General Account Settings page (see Figure 2.2).

Figure 2.2: Account Settings Page

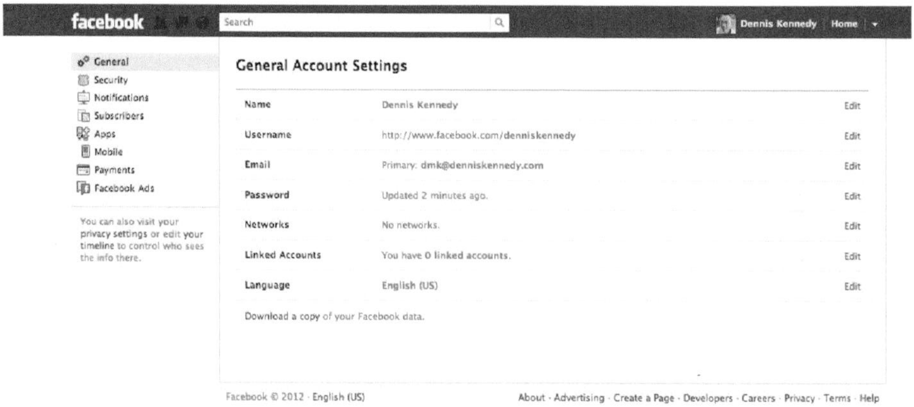

Facebook has made it easy to manage your account settings in one place. In the left column, you'll see all the areas in which you can change settings: General, Security, Notifications, Subscribers, Apps, Mobile, Payments, and Facebook Ads. Simply click on one of these items and you'll be taken to a page where you can adjust the relevant settings. We recommend that you take the time to explore all of these, but we'll highlight the most important ones to get you started.

General Settings

The General Settings page lets you check and edit the most basic account settings: Name, Username, E-mail, Password, Networks,

Linked Accounts, and Language. You will also see a link to a tool that allows you to download your Facebook data so you can keep your own archive of your Facebook data, including photos and video, with some notable exceptions—for example, Friends' photos and Updates, Comments you've made on Friends' posts and Friends' e-mail addresses and other personal information.

These settings are fairly self-explanatory. As a general matter, you will want to use your real name—the one that you use in the real world—on Facebook. The Name setting lets you make changes, such as adding or removing a middle name or initial or using a shortened name (e.g., Bill instead of William). Use the name by which people know you best. Facebook allows you to change your Name only once.

The E-mail setting allows you to change your primary e-mail address setting. If you've used a work e-mail address, you might want to change to a personal Gmail, Hotmail, or other web-based e-mail address you expect to keep for a long time.

A great feature of the Password setting is that it tells you the last time you changed your password or if you've ever changed it. It's a great reminder to refresh your password occasionally (remember to use strong passwords—a combination of upper- and lowercase letters, numbers, and symbols).

The Networks settings relate to Facebook Networks that you can join, such as your college, high school, geographic location, or the like. Sometimes being part of a network might seem like a good idea, but it might also make you more visible or findable than you might like.

Security Settings

Any time you spend configuring your security settings is time well spent. Again, Facebook's layout makes it easy to walk through these settings and adjust them to suit your needs.

The categories are Secure Browsing, Login Notifications, Login Approvals, App Passwords, Recognized Devices, and Active Sessions (see Figure 2.3). You can also deactivate your account from this page. Note that Facebook's definition of "deactivation" is different from "deletion." "Deactivation" means that Facebook expects you to come back and use your account. "Deletion," which can take a while to accomplish, means that you never want to come back.

Figure 2.3: Security Settings Page

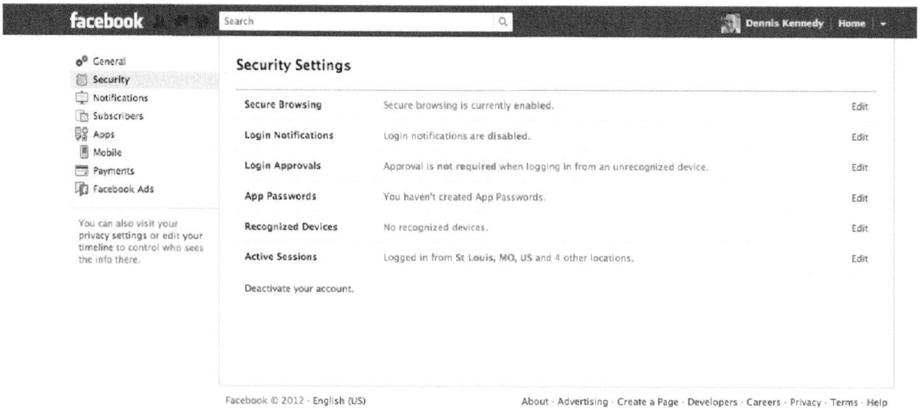

Secure Browsing is quite an important category, especially if you ever use Facebook over public WiFi. Click on the edit icon and check the box to enable secure browsing. Facebook will then use the secure HTTP protocol. You'll know it by the *https://* in the browser address bar, which may be familiar from your online banking, shopping, and other secure websites. In simplest terms, this setting will prevent people from gaining access to your Facebook account while you are in a coffee shop or other place where you use public WiFi. We can't think of any reason you would not want to enable this setting.

The other security settings allow you to get notice of or have control over logins, specify the devices that may access your Facebook account, and simlar functions so you can be aware of anyone else's attempts to access your account. We recommend that you explore each of these settings and set up the features that make sense for you. For example, if you are concerned someone else is using your account, you might want to enable login notifications.

Notifications

Facebook gives you a lot of control over the notifications you get about activities in Facebook and the ability to customize those settings (see Figure 2.4).

Figure 2.4: Notification Settings Page

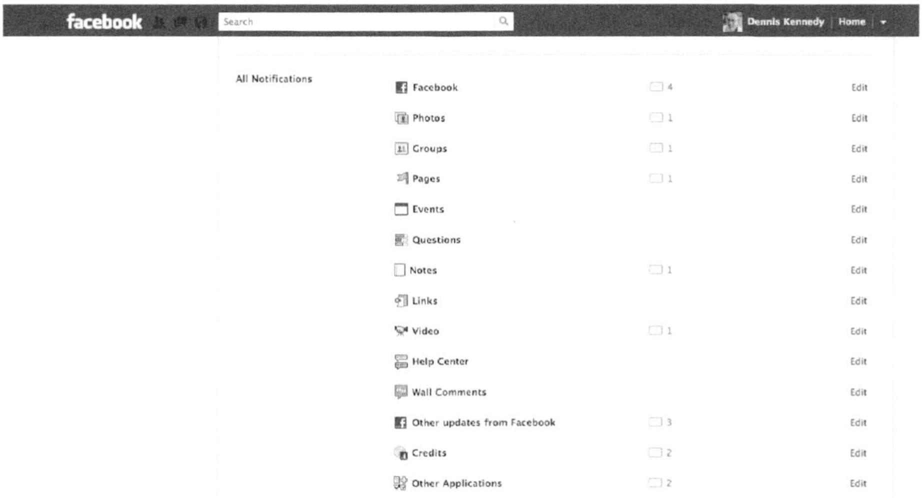

Note the many areas for which you can customize notification settings. You can get a summary e-mail of all your notifications rather than individual e-mails. We discuss notifications in more detail in Lesson 9.

Other Settings

Take a few minutes and work through all of the other settings shown in the left column in Figure 2.2. Even if you aren't yet familiar with Facebook, you'll get a good idea of how much you can do and the many ways you can customize your experience.

The category we especially want to highlight is Apps (see Figure 2.5).

Figure 2.5: App Settings Page

Many Facebook users are surprised by the number of apps that have access to their accounts. We discuss Apps in detail in the Advanced Topics section of this book. You might add an app and forget about it or give an app access to certain data without fully realizing it. The Apps settings page is a great tool to let you see which apps have access to your account or data and to remove apps or adjust the access rights they have. Many apps let you give permission for them to post to your Facebook account as if they were you. It can be an unsettling feeling when you find that you are updating Facebook as you listen to songs or watch videos.

Privacy Settings

Privacy Settings in Facebook are extremely important. In general, it's probably best to use restrictive privacy settings to start and then gradually open them up, if you want, as you better understand Facebook, your audience, your use, and the data you plan to share.

As with the Account Settings, you'll enter the Privacy Settings under the Home button on the top blue navigation bar (see Figure 2.1). After you click on the "Privacy Settings" item, you'll see the main Privacy Settings page (see Figure 2.6).

Figure 2.6: Privacy Settings Page

We recommend that you work your way through all the privacy settings in the same way we did for the account settings. One of the great improvements Facebook has made over the years on privacy is collecting all of the privacy settings in one place. We think that

Facebook users, especially lawyers, who see the Privacy Settings page will feel much better about privacy than they have in the past.

The Privacy Settings page starts with an important explanation about the granular control Facebook gives you to set the audience when you post status Updates, photos, and other information. It also explains that the people with whom you share can share that information with others—just as they can in real-world interactions.

Next, you have the ability to set a default privacy setting. There are three choices: Public, Friends, and Custom. Public means everyone can see. We do mean everyone, including non-Facebook members, which might become a much bigger issue if search engines index these public posts. The best approach is to set this for Friends initially and then consider whether a Custom approach makes sense later as you learn how you use Facebook.

Next, you will see five categories of settings, all of which are important.

How You Connect

To manage how you connect to people, click on the Edit Settings link and a box will pop up with three areas you can adjust (see Figure 2.7). There's also a handy **Learn more** link if you want more information.

Figure 2.7: How You Connect Settings Menu

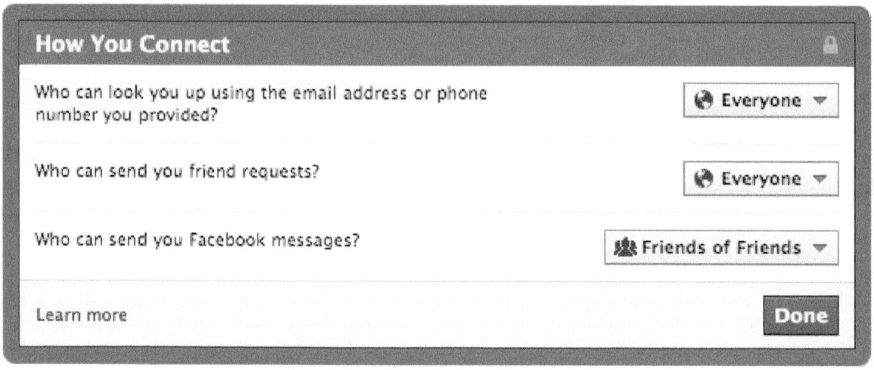

36

Each category has three choices: Everyone, Friends of Friends, and Friends. Limiting each category to **Friends** may seem like a good idea, but this approach probably does not make sense for every category. After all, how would you get new Friend requests or let others reach you if these categories are limited to Friends? Reasonable choices for these categories are Everyone or Friends of Friends. If you want to be cautious and see how much unsolicited contact you get through Facebook, then start with Friends of Friends. You can always go back and change the settings.

Timelines and Tagging

These privacy settings (farther down the page shown in Figure 2.6) let you manage what happens when Friends "tag" you or your content, or post on your Timeline (see Figure 2.8). In other words, they let you control how actions your Friends take on Facebook might affect your

Figure 2.8: Timelines and Tagging Settings

privacy. We talk about Tags and Timelines later in the book (Timelines in Lesson 3 and Tags in Lesson 7), so you'll want to revisit these settings when you have a good understanding of these features.

Each of these categories addresses something that someone else can do that will show up on your Timeline or otherwise be visible to others. The last category covers Facebook's ability to use its facial recognition software to suggest a tag identifying you in another person's photo when they post it to Facebook. That increases your risk of being identified in an embarrassing photo, even where you might be an innocent bystander. Although Facebook's facial recognition program is apparently quite good, you do have a risk of misidentification.

Until you are familiar with these features, we recommend that you use a heavy hand in configuring these settings, limiting your settings to Friends, and enabling the pre-review features. We're not comfortable with allowing the tag suggestion feature for photos, but you might be.

Apps, Games, and Websites

As we mentioned above, people are often very surprised at how games and apps use their Facebook data. As a result, we think these settings are especially important. Click on **Edit Settings for Apps, Games, and Websites** (farther down the page shown in Figure 2.6) and you'll see a pop-up screen for configuring the settings (see Figure 2.9).

You know the drill by now. Just work your way through each of the categories and edit where appropriate.

Limit the Audience for Past Posts

We expect some of you to start cheering when you see this category. It's possible that you've posted something on Facebook in the past that

Figure 2.9: Apps, Games, and Websites Settings Page

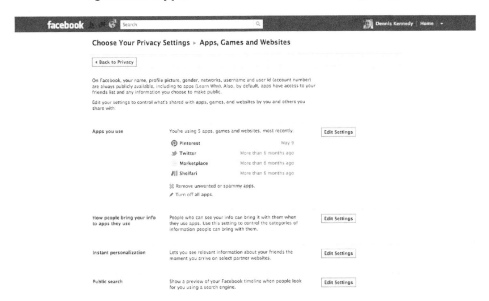

you would prefer that people could not access anymore. The good news is that Facebook now helps you with that.

Move farther down the page shown in Figure 2.6 to the link for **Limit Audience for Old Posts**. The pop-up menu will give you options and more useful information about these important issues (see Figure 2.10).

Figure 2.10: Limit Audience for Old Posts Pop-Up

Essentially, Facebook gives you an easy way to go back and limit to Friends the audience for postings where the audience settings were either Public or Friends of Friends. This feature might be hugely beneficial to someone who did not understand privacy settings and is now looking for a job, for example. Lawyers might also see some potential issues with this feature in a litigation setting, especially in the context of litigation hold. Note that you can also make changes to the visibility of individual entries on your Timeline.

Blocked People and Apps

While this category, found farther down the page shown in Figure 2.6, might initially seem like the "nuclear option," it actually offers powerful ways to deal with some Facebook annoyances. Again, click open the pop-up and work through the choices. You can restrict a Friend to seeing only your Public postings, block app invites from your Farmville-playing Friends by app or by Friend, or block individual apps. These options are especially valuable if you have Friends who send you lots of game invitations.

Knowing What Other People Can See

Facebook users often run into privacy issues because they don't understand what other people can see or because certain data can be more revealing than they expect. The great "View As" tool allows you to see exactly how your Facebook presence appears to others. Simply go to your **Timeline** by clicking on your name in the top blue navigation bar, click on the **gear icon** under your Cover Photo, and click on the **View As . . .** option. You will see what the public sees when they view your Timeline (see Figure 2.11).

Figure 2.11: View As Public Sees

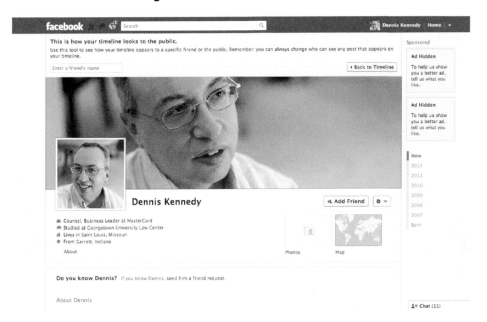

Near the top is a search box where you can type in a name to see how your Timeline is displayed to a specific person. It should be readily apparent how valuable this tool can be.

A Few Conclusions

As we go through the remaining Lessons, we'll revisit some of the privacy and security settings when we discuss specific Facebook features. We'll also discuss other granular settings in the context of the features they affect.

If you spend a few minutes doing what we cover in this Lesson, you'll easily be among the savviest Facebook users—lawyers or otherwise—in terms of privacy and security. Most Facebook users simply have no idea about what's happening with their data, how it can be accessed, or how they can change their settings. If we've been successful with this Lesson, you should feel reasonably comfortable about Facebook privacy and what you can do to protect your privacy.

In Lesson 3, we launch into the basic features, starting with the Profile and the Timeline.

Creating Your Profile and Managing Your Timeline

What Is a Facebook Profile?

Individuals create Profiles, and businesses (for example, law firms) create Pages. We cover Pages in more depth in the next Lesson. For now, we're talking about personal Profiles because, at its heart, any networking you do, whether online or off-line, is about developing and nurturing relationships with individuals. People do business with people.

We consider Profiles one of the three essentials of Facebook, i.e., your Identity. Your Profile is all about you as an individual—your bio, your educational and work history, your personal photos, and your likes and dislikes, from music to movies and more. Your Profile is like a personal website; it's the equivalent of combining the Home and About pages of a standard website. Once you have entered the Profile information, it becomes the foundation for your Timeline (formerly known as the Wall). The Timeline is where people on Facebook initially go to interact with you, and it is where they will land when they search for you on Facebook.

Note that the Facebook platform is increasingly emphasizing the Timeline. We expect that the Profile will gradually merge with the Timeline and that there will not be a meaningful distinction between them. We use the term Profile in this Lesson, but your Facebook Profile is actually not housed in one specific location on Facebook; it is made up of pieces of information that can be accessed from the Timeline. For example, your About information is part of your Profile and is accessible from the Timeline, but not all of your About information can be seen directly from the Timeline. Most users, especially new users, will think in terms of Timelines. To keep it simple, when we use the term "Profile," we mean the information you provide to Facebook about yourself. The page you find when you click on your name in the top blue navigation bar is your Timeline, which you can consider as the publicly facing version of your Profile.

Lawyers and Profiles

You can share as much or as little personal information as you want on Facebook, but always keep in mind those privacy and security concerns we discussed in Lesson 2, as well as ethical issues that may arise (which we will discuss in Advanced Topics). As a lawyer, those ethical issues can apply to your personal Profile and Timeline just as they can to your law firm Page.

We recommend that you create a Profile even if you intend to use Facebook solely for business and just want a Page for your solo practice or small law firm. You don't need to post updates on your Profile or fill it with much information. A Profile gives you many more options and much more functionality on the Pages that you administer than if you create a Page without a personal Profile attached (Facebook calls these business accounts).

Creating Your Profile and Timeline

Even though Facebook considers Step 1 to be finding Friends, we're going to skip this step because we think it makes more sense to have a more complete Profile before inviting others to be your Friend. (We'll discuss Friending and finding Friends in Lesson 5.)

A complete Profile helps people who look for you on Facebook more easily recognize who you are and—we hope—respond to your Friend invitations faster. More importantly, a complete Profile increases the likelihood that Friends will begin to *interact* with you on Facebook, which is the point. Social and professional networking and establishing relationships require interaction.

If security is one of your main concerns and you prefer to use Facebook primarily for business relationships, complete only the very basic information required to open your account. We recommend that you add a little information to your Profile and Timeline even if you restrict who can see it because personal interaction (networking) helps develop and generate business.

Most people's first contact with you on Facebook will be your Timeline, which is based on your Profile. People may find you through a Facebook suggestion or because they uploaded their e-mail contacts, or you invited them to be your Friend. When they click on your name or photo they are taken to your Timeline. But after the initial contact most of the interaction between you and your Friends is more likely to occur in their News Feeds or through private Messages (we'll discuss them in Lessons 7 and 8).

To get to your Timeline, click on your name in the blue bar at the top of any Facebook screen (see Figure 3.1).

What Should the Profile and Timeline Contain?

Many lawyers are familiar with LinkedIn, which puts a big emphasis on creating a professional, résumé-like Profile that identifies you and provides a lot of information about you in one place in a structured format. Like LinkedIn, Facebook controls the structure and design of

Figure 3.1: Facebook Timeline

your Timeline, but you control the content. The amount of content on Profiles and Timelines may vary, but it appears in the same place and in the same way for every Facebook user.

User Profiles and Timelines are, by definition, personal and you can control who sees what on your Profile and Timeline. (As we'll see in Lesson 4, this differs from Pages, which are public.) Profiles and Timelines are specific to one individual, and each individual can have only one personal Profile, identified by your first and last name. If you have a common name, you might want to add your middle name or initial to differentiate yourself from someone else who has the same name.

Keep in mind that businesses, including law firms, should create Pages, not Profiles. Your Profile is just for you. Although you can talk about what your firm does or what you are doing in the legal world on your Timeline, you can't create a personal Profile for The Smith Law Firm. The Personal Profile has to be John M. Smith; if Facebook finds a Profile for a business, it can be removed, and you may not be able to retrieve it or its content.

Building Your Profile

Initially, Facebook will ask you for three pieces of information: your high school, your college, and your employer. As with most fields (except your name and e-mail address), you can choose not to complete any of these fields, but we recommend that you do because colleagues and classmates will be able to find you more easily.

Once you have completed this basic information, press **Save and Continue**. Facebook will likely suggest that you **Add People You Know**. These Friend suggestions are based on the information you just entered. You may choose to add these Friends if you know them, but for now we will skip this step, so press **Skip**.

Your Profile Picture

Next, Facebook requests that you upload a Profile Picture, a small (thumbnail) image that others see when they interact with you. Although many people choose images that include other people (or even pets), we recommend that for maximum recognition you use a photo that is mostly your face. You can upload an existing photo from your computer or, in a pinch, you can take a photo directly from your computer's webcam by clicking on the **Take a Photo** link on the screen (although the result won't be as professional).

If you choose to upload a photo, click on the **Upload a Photo** link and then **Choose File** and navigate to the photo you would like to upload. Click **OK**. Your Profile Picture will be seen by everyone with whom you interact directly or indirectly, so be sure that it is professional and appropriate for all audiences. After you have uploaded your photo, you can crop it to improve how it looks.

If you want to change your photo, hover your mouse pointer over it and click on **Edit Profile Picture**. You can then choose from existing photos you've uploaded to Facebook, take a photo with your webcam, upload a new photo, edit the thumbnail image, or remove the picture. If you remove or do not choose a Profile photo, Facebook will put a placeholder image there that appears as a silhouette of a person. At best a blank silhouette image creates a negative impression, and it might even make people wonder if you are in a witness protection program.

The Cover Photo

Facebook recently rolled out the new Timeline format, which includes not only a Profile photo, but also a Cover Photo—a large photograph that is displayed across the top of your Timeline, similar to the header on a website. The Cover Photo can be a photograph of you, your family, a hobby, or almost anything you can think of. It should be at least 399 pixels wide, but Facebook will stretch a regular photo to fit the cover dimensions.

To add your Cover Photo, hover your mouse pointer over the Cover Photo area and a pop-up menu will appear. It will allow you to upload a new photo or choose from existing photos you have already uploaded to Facebook.

Once you have chosen or uploaded a Cover Photo, you can reposition it within the frame on your Timeline. When you are satisfied with the way the photo appears, click **Save Changes**. You can change your Cover Photo as often as you like.

Next Steps

After your initial photos are set, Facebook takes you to your Home page. When your account is very new, your Home page displays a Facebook Welcome. Click on the **Edit Profile** button at the top of the page to continue building your Profile.

If you no longer see the Welcome page but want to edit your Profile, you can do so from your Timeline. Click the **Update Info** button on the right below your Cover Photo. From your Home page, you can also edit your Profile and Timeline by clicking on your name in the blue navigation bar at the top of the page, or by clicking on your name or picture at the top left corner of the screen, immediately under the Facebook logo.

Other Photos

Given that Facebook is such a visual medium, photos are one of the most often shared items, and can trigger the most interactions.

In addition to the Cover Photo and Profile photo, you can add other personal photos. From your **Timeline**, click **Update Info** and navigate to the drop-down box next to your name. Click **About** and choose **Photos** (see Figure 3.2).

Facebook takes you to a page with your cover and profile photos and any other photos you have uploaded. Below these are photos in which you have been "tagged" (we'll cover tagging in Lesson 7), and they appear under Photos of You (see Figure 3.3).

Figure 3.2: Update Drop-Down Menu

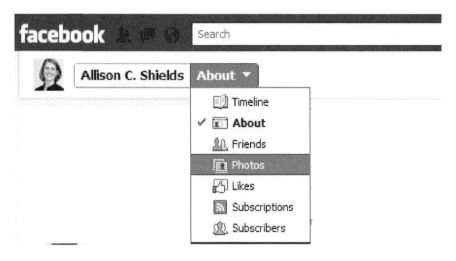

Figure 3.3: Photos

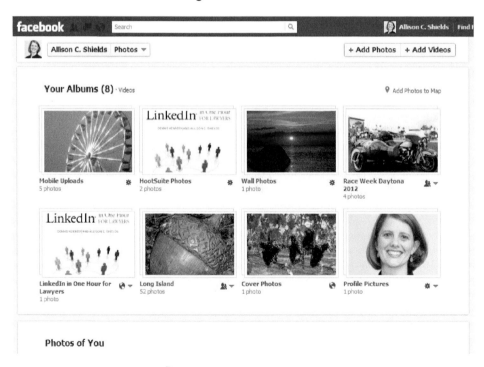

To change your Profile Picture, follow the same steps as you did to upload it originally. To add more Photos or Videos, click on the appropriate button in the upper right: **Add Photos+** or **Add Videos+** (see Figure 3.3).

You can access your Photos and Videos by clicking on the **Photos** box in the strip at the top of your Timeline and beneath your Cover Photo (See Figure 3.1). All the tabs at the top of your Timeline work this way: click **Friends** for a list of your Friends, and so on.

About

Under your Profile Picture is information that you entered when you created your account (where you studied, where you work, and your birthdate if you have chosen to share that information). This is your About information. Compared to LinkedIn, the information is rather bare bones.

To view more details, click on the **About** link under the basic bio information (or from the Timeline, click on **Update Info**). To add or update this information, click on the little **Edit** buttons next to each section (see Figure 3.4).

To the right of the Work and Education box is History by Year, which is automatically populated from history information that you provided. For example, you can see Allison's start and end dates for college and employment. This feature gives her Friends a good summary of her history. Below that section is About You, which can be completed with additional information.

As you edit each section, you will see a small icon with a downward pointing arrow at the upper right of the editing box. This icon allows you to decide who can see each section. Most fields will default to Public (a globe icon), but you can change that so only Friends or specific groups of Friends can see specific information. Don't forget to click **Save** when you finish adding or changing the content.

Figure 3.4: About

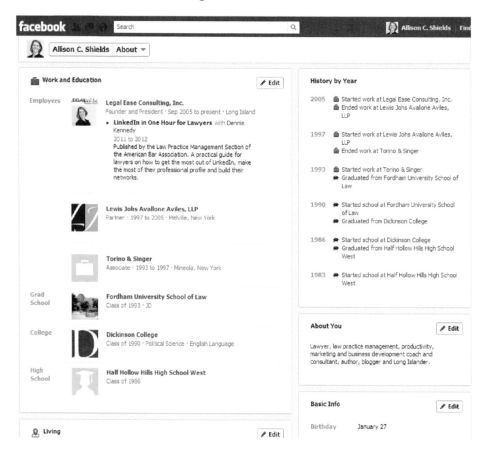

Map

The **Map** shows where you've checked in on Facebook (see Lesson 7 for more on Checking In), as well as your hometown, where you live now, and other places you've lived in the past. Life Events can also be included on your Map.

You can choose to hide the Map from your Profile if you don't want others to see where you are or where you've been, but if you've checked in at a Place on Facebook, that story will need to be separately hidden from your Timeline. Lawyers who work from home but don't meet clients there or don't want clients to know where they live (or for anyone who travels a lot and posts where and when they are traveling on Facebook) may want to think twice about using the Map feature or checking in because you'll be broadcasting on Facebook where you are (and by extension, where you are *not*).

Other Information

On the About page you can also add your contact information, relationship information, favorite quotes, and so on, setting different permissions for each as you like.

Think about what you want to publish in the Profile contact information on your Profile—particularly whether you want to publicize your your cell phone number. You can list your firm or personal website URL here, but include **http://** to ensure that it's an active link.

You can find **Birthdays** Under **Basic Info**. Sending birthday greetings is a popular Facebook tradition and, for astrology buffs, you can determine your Friends' astrological signs. If you make your birthday visible on your Profile, consider changing the default **Show my full birthday in my profile** to **Show only month and day** to protect against identity theft or to keep your age private. Of course, you may choose not to show your birthday at all in your Profile. Whether you include and display your current city and hometown is up to you and may depend upon your practice area. But for most lawyers, showing this information is a good idea because the more points of connection you have with others, the better, especially if your practice tends to attract local clients.

If you are using Facebook for business or professional purposes, consider setting your About section to **Public** so the description of what you do is indexed by Google and can be viewed by everyone on the Internet. You can also mention your firm's Page here.

Whenever you want to update information in the About section, click on the **Update Info** button beneath and to the right of your Cover Photo (see Figures 3.1 and 3.5). You can also view your activity on Facebook by clicking on the **Activity Log** button, which allows you to see all of your recent Facebook activity, including Updates, Posts, Likes, and Comments in one place.

You can add even more elements to your Profile and Timeline. After clicking on Update Info, go to the top of the page and click on the **down arrow** next to About next to your name to access an additional menu of items to choose. Click on **Likes** to see a page of all of the things you have Liked. Here you can also share some of your Favorites, which include music, books, movies, interests, television shows, sports, activities, and more. Sharing this type of information can help you show a human side (often important for a lawyer).

How much you share depends on your personal preference, although we don't recommend spending too much time filling in these categories in the beginning. Instead, you might want to add to them piecemeal, or choose one category that really appeals to you and add some information at the beginning. Be aware that as you "Like" things on Facebook (or click a Facebook "Like" button on another website), some of this information will fill in automatically.

Navigating Your Timeline

When you click on your name or picture in the blue Facebook navigation bar, you go to your Timeline. The top of your Timeline is a reference section for your Facebook activity (see Figure 3.5).

This section includes your Cover Photo, Profile Photo, name, and other basic information. Under your name and profile photo, you'll find some information pulled from the About section of your Profile. When you view your own Timeline, you may be prompted to add additional information here, such as **Add your hometown** in the About section.

Figure 3.5: Facebook Timeline

Note that each of the items in blue in your About section is a link, which is clickable. For example, if you click on Legal Ease Consulting, Inc., in Allison's About section, you'll go to Allison's Legal Ease Consulting, Inc. Page.

To the right of the About section is a series of tabs. First is the **Friends** tab with thumbnails of some of your Friends. Clicking on the tab or the name under the tab accesses a page where you can manage Friends, which we discuss in Lesson 5. Next to it is **Photos**, which accesses your photo albums.

Likes are next, and the tab displays a few of your most recent likes. Last on Allison's Timeline is the **Subscribers** tab, showing how many people subscribe to her public Updates (we'll discuss Subscriptions in Lesson 8).

In Figure 3.5, to the right of these four tabs is a number with a down arrow (in Figure 3.5, that number is *1*). That number indicates the existence of additional tabs, and clicking on the down arrow displays them. A Profile or personal Timeline can have a total of eight tabs. Allison has only five, including Friends, Photos, Likes, Subscribers, and the fifth, hidden tab that you cannot see on this view which is **Subscriptions**. Clicking on that tab accesses the lists and people she subscribes to.

Additional available tabs include **Map** and **Notes**, which Allison has not activated. The Friends and Photos tabs are always the first two, but you can change the position of the other tabs by hovering over the image on the tab and clicking on the **pencil icon** that appears.

Directly above the tabs is a row of buttons. First is the **Update Info** button, which allows you to update your basic Profile information, including work and educational experience, About, contact informtion, and so on.

Second is **Activity Log**, which only the registered user of the account can view. It shows all your recent activity, including Likes, comments on others' posts, changes to your Timeline or Profile, Status Updates, and more.

Third is the **gear icon** with the downward triangle. Clicking on the triangle provides the option to view your Timeline as if you were another Facebook user so you can see the Public view, the basic Friend view, and the view people on your different Friend lists can see. Use these views to see if you want to change any of your settings (see Figure 3.6). We discussed these settings in Lesson 2. An option

Figure 3.6: View Profile As

under the gear icon allows you to add a badge to your website or blog to promote your Facebook Profile.

Status Update Box

When viewing your own Timeline, you'll see two columns of items below the About section. At the top of the left column is the **Status Update** box that you use to update your Friends and subscribers about your activities. We'll talk more about Updates in Lesson 7.

Friends Box

To the right of the Status Update box on the Timeline is the Friends box. This box displays thumbnails of some of your Friends. Click on **See All** at the top of the box to access the Manage Friends page. (Note: when you view someone else's Timeline, an indicator in the Friends box tells you how many Friends you have in common.)

Recent Activity

Directly below the Friends box, you'll see a Recent Activity box, which lists your most recent activities.

Hovering over the top of the Recent Activity will bring up a **pencil icon.** Clicking on the icon allows you to edit or remove recent activity. You can also hover over individual posts and remove them from your recent activity by clicking on the *x* that appears to the right of the post.

Friends Added

Beneath Recent Activity is **Friends Added,** which shows thumbnails of the Friends you've added in the current month. Hovering your mouse over the portion of this box that indicates the number of Friends recently added brings up the pencil icon, on which you can click for a number of options.

The Like Box

Your Timeline may also display a box similar to the Friends Added box, which displays your Likes during the current month. Once again, hovering over the top of the box will bring up the pencil icon, allowing you to view each Like individually or to hide Likes from your Timeline.

Updates/Stories

Below all of the boxes mentioned above are the posts (Facebook calls them "stories") on your Timeline displayed in chronological order. You can add items that occurred in the past, and Facebook will automatically post them at the correct point on your Timeline. For more on sharing stories, see Lesson 8.

At-a-Glance Timeline

At the far right on your Timeline is the at-a-glance timeline (Figure 3.7), which allows you to jump quickly to other dates on your Timeline or anyone else's.

As you can see, the Facebook Profile is very different from the LinkedIn Profile; Facebook emphasizes personal interests, while LinkedIn focuses on your professional résumé and accomplishments. Because of this difference, many people believe that LinkedIn is for a professional presence and Facebook is for a personal presence. But that doesn't mean that lawyers can't use Facebook for business development and professional connections. Facebook is adding features that appeal to professionals and that let you combine both the personal and professional, and we'll highlight these as we come to them throughout the book.

One of the best ways to use Facebook for professional purposes is by creating a Page for your firm. We cover that in Lesson 4.

Figure 3.7: At-a-Glance Timeline

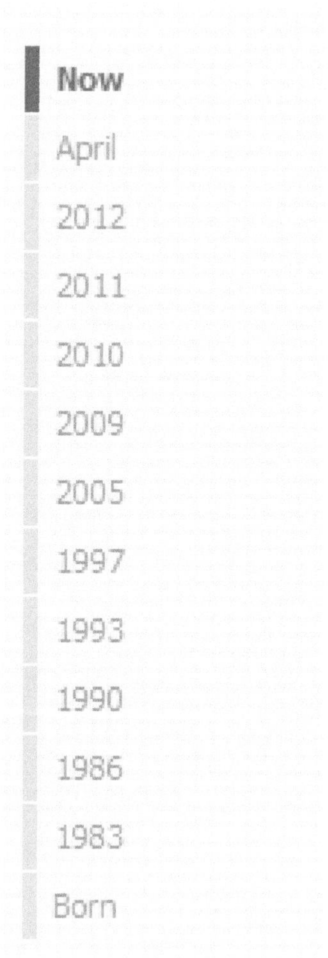

Now

April

2012

2011

2010

2009

2005

1997

1993

1990

1986

1983

Born

Establishing a Page for Your Firm or Practice

Facebook Pages, created by businesses or organizations, used to be called Fan Pages; to interact with a Page, you had to first become a Fan of it. Rather than becoming a Fan, individuals (or other Pages) can Like a Page to interact with and receive Updates from that Page. Unlike Profiles, which are limited to 5,000 Friends, Pages can have an unlimited number of followers.

Facebook encourages businesses to use Pages to help establish their business presence. Over the past several years, it has added features and tools suited for businesses, and we expect Pages to continue to improve. If you want a Facebook presence for your law firm or solo practice, Pages provide many benefits.

Creating Your Page

Before you create a Page for your law firm, make sure the firm has authorized you to do so.

To create a Page, click on Pages and Ads from your Home Page bookmarks, then click Create a Page. You can also click Create a Page from the footer on Facebook or go to **http://www.facebook.com/ pages/create.php**. Any of these actions will take you to a page like Figure 4.1.

Figure 4.1: Create Page

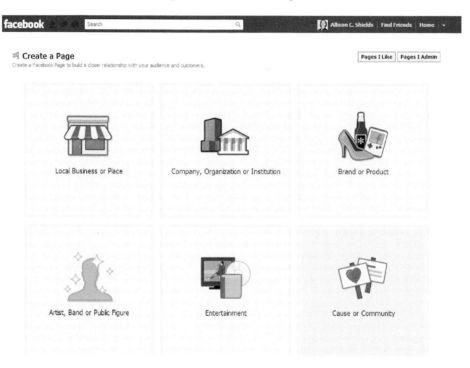

Let's assume that you are creating a Page for your firm. Click on **Company, Organization or Institution**, and then choose a category for your Page (see Figure 4.2). Next, choose a name for your Page. Think carefully about the name of your Page. You can change it, but only until you have reached 100 "Likes" on the Page—then the name becomes permanent.

Like Profiles, Pages feature a Cover Photo, which is at least 399 pixels wide (Facebook recommends 815 × 315 pixels) and a smaller Profile Picture, which is 180 pixels square. These images appear at the top of your Timeline. Upload these images as you did for your Profile in Lesson 3. Most often, the Profile Picture will be your firm's logo, but if you are a solo practitioner, you might want to use your head-

Figure 4.2: Categories

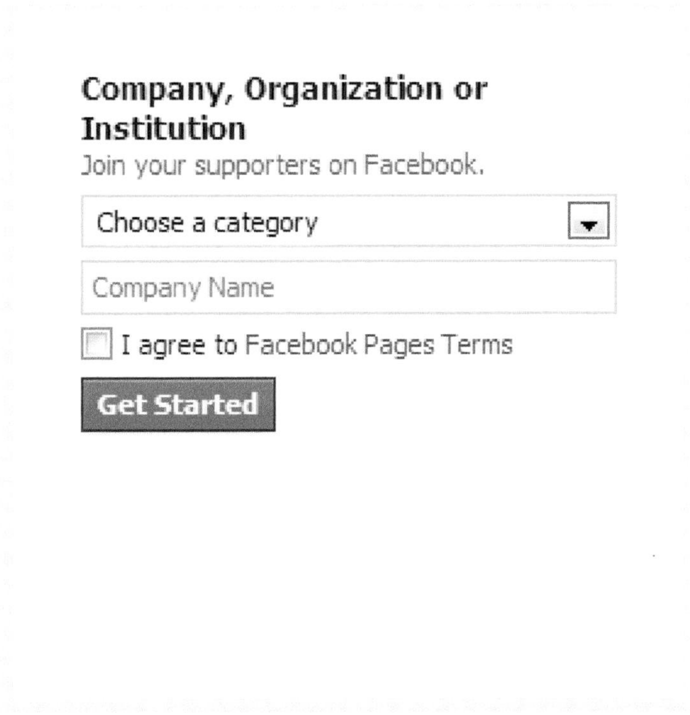

Company, Organization or Institution

Join your supporters on Facebook.

> Choose a category ▼
>
> Company Name
>
> ☐ I agree to Facebook Pages Terms
>
> **Get Started**

shot. Think of your Cover Photo like a header on your website—it's large and it spans the top of the site.

Facebook has imposed several rules on Cover Photos, mostly to combat common promotional tactics deemed inappropriate for the default landing page for a business. Here are some of the things that are now prohibited in Page Cover Photos:

- a call to action
- a Like button
- a lot of text
- links to your website
- contact information
- price/fee information

You can create a Page without having a personal Profile, but we recommend that you designate a Page Administrator with a Profile to create the Page. Once the Page is created, you can add and delete administrators or change their role and their level of control over the Page.

Many more features and options are available to registered Facebook users than to business account holders who have no personal Profile. If you set up a business account and do not create a personal Profile to act as the Page Administrator, you will be able to view, edit, and add content to your Page, run ads related to the Page, and view Page statistics, but you will not be able to interact with other Pages, view others' content, send or receive Friend requests, be found in searches, add apps to your account, or develop any Facebook apps, all of which you can do if you also have a personal Profile.

Although the Page Administrator does not have to be a lawyer, the Page must abide by the ethical rules of your jurisdiction (see Advanced Topics), and only the Administrator(s) will have access to certain functions. For these reasons, choose a highly trusted individual(s) as the Page Administrator(s), and if one of the Page Administrators leaves the firm, remove that person as a Page Administrator.

Adding Details to Your Page

Others cannot see your Page until you publish it, so you can work on it before it goes live. We recommend that you work through the following items before publishing a Page. If you have already published your Page without doing so, go back and update your Page accordingly. We'll use Allison's Legal Ease Consulting Page as our example (see Figure 4.3).

About Section/Summary Box
The About section allows for a small amount of text directly below the Profile Picture, but more can be seen when the **About** link is clicked.

Figure 4.3: Facebook Business Page

(The information is the content that used to be in the Info tab before the change to the Timeline format.)

About is front and center in the new layout, but there's only room for a small amount of text, so make it count. You might use your tagline or elevator pitch and your contact information (such as phone number, website, or blog) at the top. Next, you might include any necessary disclaimers or meet other requirements under applicable ethical rules.

To edit this section, click on **About** under your Profile Photo and brief description, hover your mouse pointer over the About section, and click the **pencil icon.** You'll be taken to a page that looks like Figure 4.4.

Timeline Apps (Formerly Page Tabs)

This section appears on the right beneath the Cover Photo. Figure 4.5 shows the Apps on Allison's Legal Ease Consulting Page. They are labeled Photos, Free Report, Welcome, and JD Supra Documents. You can include up to twelve Apps, but just as on a personal Timeline, only

Figure 4.4: Editing Your About Page Details

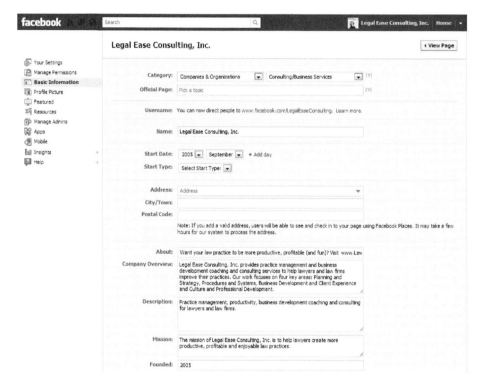

the top four Apps show automatically. The others appear only when you click on the down arrow to the right of this section. On Figure 4.5 it appears next to the number 6, indicating that the Legal Ease Consulting Page has a total of six Apps. (These Apps used to appear along the left sidebar of the old Fan Pages.)

Figure 4.5: Page Timeline Apps

With the exception of Photos, you you can change the name, order, and image of these Apps. To edit an App, hover your mouse pointer over the image and click on the **pencil icon** to access **Edit settings**. Note that the recommended size for App button images is 111 × 74 pixels.

You can use Apps as calls to action. For example, if you offer free information or downloads, you can direct Facebook visitors to your website by creating a custom App. Upload an appropriate image and a link that directs visitors to a landing page you designate. An example in Figure 4.5 is Allison's **Free Report** button, which directs visitors to her white paper and newsletter sign-up page.

The Timeline

The Timeline is where every visitor to your Page lands. Previously, Facebook allowed Pages to include a Welcome Page, which many companies used as a way to create "Like" gates—essentially blocking the content on their Page until the visitor clicked **Like**. Now visitors can see all of the content on your timeline, and as of now, there is no way you can change that.

If your firm had a pre-Timeline Welcome Page, have no fear—it still exists, and you can keep it if you want to; it just won't be the landing page. It is in the Apps section (see Allison's Welcome App in Figure 4.5).

The Timeline is just that—a timeline for your practice. Visitors to most firms are more likely to be interested in what's current at your firm than in its history, but feel free to add backdated information. You can use photos and the Timeline to tell a compelling visual story about the history and mission of the firm or your career. Facebook uses the date the event occurred or the date the photograph was taken to place it on the Timeline.

Consider these ways to use your Timeline:

■ Create **Milestones**, which are to Pages what Life Events are to personal Profiles (see Lesson 8 for more on Life Events). Milestones are designated with a flag icon and are the full width of the page (843 × 403 pixels), rather than the smaller size of regular posts (520 pixels wide). A Milestone must include a title, but it can also include other details. Mergers, office moves, and the addition of a new partner are events you might want to include as Milestones.

■ **Star** stories to expand the post to widescreen and make it more prominent.

■ **Pin** a post to the top of your Timeline for up to a week: after that, it returns to its chronological place in the Timeline.

■ **Backdate** posts for special events in the life of your firm that occurred before you started your Page.

■ **Schedule** posts to appear on your Timeline in the future. This new feature allows you to create several posts at once and spread out their appearance over time.

When you hover your mouse pointer over a post in the Timeline, you will see a **pencil icon**, which allows you to pin or hide a post or change the post date. You can mark new posts as Milestones right from the Status Update box.

Friend Activity

Visitors to your Page Timeline see Friend Activity. For example, they see which of their Friends have Liked your Page, and if one of their Friends has tagged or linked to a post from your Page, it will be highlighted.

Interacting with Others Using Your Page

When others Like your Page, they can interact with the Page in several ways if the features are enabled: join discussions, comment on posts, respond to poll questions, and share links and photos. Alternatively, the Page Administrator can choose to allow only the Page Administrator(s) to post to the Page.

Everything that is posted to a Page is considered Public, so it can be seen by anyone. Google indexes Pages (another good reason to create and post on a Page). Page Administrators may remove posts and comments or ban individuals from posting on their Page altogether if they consider the posts to be off-topic or offensive. These bans are limited to the Page in question and do not prohibit the individual from posting on the Pages of other businesses.

Increasing Page Interaction

Most visitors will encounter your Timeline only the first time they come to your Page. After that, they'll see your posts in their News Feed—but only occasionally. For those reasons, one of the main complaints we hear from Page Administrators is that Facebook has made interacting with their audience difficult without using paid ads or Sponsored Stories (discussed at the end of this Lesson).

Facebook does not automatically push every Update to Page subscribers' News Feeds, so if you want to interact with your audience, you'll have to think of ways to make your Page and Timeline destinations that are worth visiting repeatedly. Of course, those who want to follow your Page can create an Interest List, add your Page to that list, and ensure that the list is marked All Updates so that they receive all of your posts, but you have no control over that. Even so, we think creating a Page for a law firm of any size makes sense for marketing purposes, to build relationships, and to keep everyone in the firm aware of what is happening at the firm.

Messages

The Message button, which is below the cover photo on the right, allows viewers to send a private Message within Facebook to your Page, and your Admin Panel at the top of your Page is where you can see those Messages. We don't know whether or how often clients or potential clients will attempt to contact firms through the Message button on the Page. Suffice it to say that if you create a Page for your firm, you'll need to ensure that someone is checking these messages frequently (and depending on your jurisdiction's ethical rules, you may need a disclaimer as well; for more on disclaimers, see the Ethics discussion in Advanced Topics). If you're concerned about this issue, you can change your Page settings to uncheck the box that allows Messages.

Managing Your Page

Privacy and Permissions Settings

As the creator or administrator of your Page, you have some options for managing content on the Page (see Figure 4.6).

Facebook's Help Center has this to say about Post Visibility and Pages:

> Posts about a Page respect the privacy settings of the people who create them. *Page admins won't see posts about their Page that people haven't shared publicly even though people visiting the Page might see them if they're part of the audience the post was shared with. Pages themselves are public spaces,* and posts added to a Page's Timeline will be visible publicly and are eligible to appear in the Recent Posts by Others box (emphasis added).

Figure 4.6: Manage Page Permissions

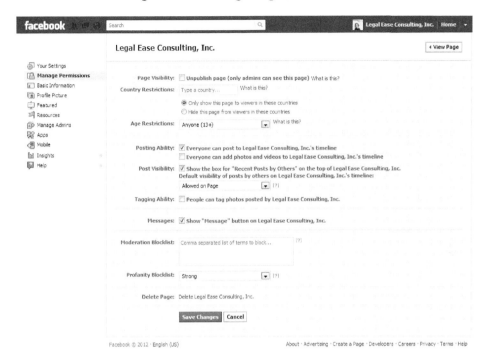

Keep in mind that Facebook considers your Page to be a public space when setting the permissions for your page. As noted above, posts *about* your Page posted elsewhere on Facebook may not always be visible to the Page Administrator, depending on the settings chosen by the person creating the post. But Page Administrators can control what is posted *on* their Page; you can choose to review posts before they can appear on your Page's Timeline, to prohibit others' posts on your Page, and to turn off the Recent Posts by Others box on your Page's timeline. At the very least, we recommend that all lawyers set these permissions to allow posts by others only after they have been approved by the Page Administrator.

To prevent posts by others from appearing on your Page's Timeline until you review them, go to the **Manage** menu in your Admin Panel to get to the Page Permissions (Figure 4.6) and select **Edit Page**. Next to Post Visibility, choose **Hidden from Page** from the drop-down box. Then visit the Activity Log to view others' posts and determine whether to show them on your Page's Timeline.

You can also choose not to show any posts by others, but that will inhibit interaction with your Page, so think about your Page's purpose when setting these permissions. If you choose not to permit posts by others, **uncheck the boxes** on the permissions page next to "Everyone can post to . . ." and "Everyone can add photos and videos to . . ."

Hiding a post from your Page removes it from your Page's Timeline so people won't see it there. You can choose to unhide it later from your activity log. Photos you've hidden from your Page's Timeline are still visible when people access your Page's Photos view, unless you delete the photo entirely. To hide a post on your Timeline, go to the **pencil icon** by hovering over the post and select **Hide from Page**. To permanently delete a post, select **Delete Post** (Facebook will ask you to confirm).

Regardless of your Page settings, visitors to your Page will still see posts about how their Friends have interacted with your Page (the Friend Activity mentioned previously).

The creator or administrator of your firm's Page does not need to be made Public, and if it's not, none of the administrator's personal information will be seen by those viewing the Page. But Facebook does allow Page owners and administrators to designate Featured Owners of the Page, so the featured owner's personal information will display in the Page's About section, and the Page will be displayed on the featured owner's personal Profile. This setting might be good for solos and small firms. Review the Page guidelines at: **http://www.facebook.com/page_guidelines.php.**

Admin Panel

The Admin Panel is where you'll go to approve posts made by others to your Page (if you have allowed that in your Page Permissions) and where you can find your notifications in an easy-to-read format. Once you have at least twenty-five Likes, you will also see Page Insights here. From the Admin Panel you can access your Activity Log and the Edit menu, from which you can make changes to your Page's settings, including post visibility and permissions.

Page Administrators

As we were in the process of writing this book, Facebook rolled out new controls for Administrators. Now there are five different roles for Page Administrators: Manager, Content Creator, Moderator, Advertiser, and Insights Analyst. Each of these roles has a different level of permissions, with Manager having the most and Insights Analyst the least. Search "administrator roles" in the Facebook Help Center to find out more.

Publicizing Your Page

Inviting Page Likes

You can invite only confirmed Friends to Like your Page, but if you have a personal Profile associated with your Page, you can choose to send invitations to some of those Friends if you think they might be interested in your Page. This is another reason to associate a personal Profile with your firm's Page.

To invite Friends to your Page, go to the Page's Admin Panel, click **Build Audience**, and select **Invite Friends**. You can choose a list or All Friends. Check the boxes next to those you want to invite and click **Submit**.

Facebook Badges and Like Buttons

Get a Facebook badge for your existing firm website or blog to direct visitors to your Page in Facebook. You can get a badge at http://www.facebook.com/badges/page.php.

You can also add Like buttons to your website or blog. Although this won't drive traffic to your Page, it will help your website visitors share your content with their Friends; when they Like a blog post or a page on your firm's website, their Like appears on their Timeline.

Facebook Ads

You can create ads for your Pages or Events that will encourage further interaction with your Page. We discuss Facebook Ads and Events in Lesson 10. When viewing the ads, people can connect directly from the ad, either Liking the Page or RSVP'ing to an Event. These actions will create a story on the viewer's Timeline and may show up in their Friends' News Feeds as well.

Sponsored Stories

If you want to highlight specific News Feed stories about interactions people have had with your Page, you can pay to create a Sponsored Story, which has a better chance of being seen in the News Feeds of the Friends of the individual highlighted in the story, giving your Page additional exposure.

Converting a Personal Profile into a Page

As we noted in Lesson 3, Facebook considers Profiles to be personal; only individuals are permitted to have Facebook Profiles. If your current "personal" Profile is really about your firm and not about you as an individual, you can—and should—convert it before Facebook finds out and removes it.

When you convert your personal Profile into a business Page, Facebook will convert all of your confirmed Friends and Subscribers into people who have Liked your page. You will become the administrator for the Page, and your username and Profile Picture will become the user name and Profile Picture for the Page. But beware—*none* of your other content, including Photos, Updates, and Profile information will be transferred to the new Page. See Facebook's help section to find out how to download that content before you convert the Page.

With your personal and professional identities complete with a Profile and a Page, you're now ready for Lesson 5 and to connect to Friends.

Friending Effectively

The main purpose of joining Facebook is to interact with others, and most of that interaction takes place with your Friends. We consider Friending as the second essential component of Facebook.

Just as with LinkedIn Connections, Friending on Facebook is reciprocal; it requires the agreement of both parties. When someone sends you a Friend request, you must confirm that request before you are confirmed Friends, and the same happens when you send a Friend request to someone else on Facebook.

Because Friending requires a bilateral acknowledgement of a relationship, you have the option of not becoming Friends with someone, just as someone you invite might decide not to become Friends with you.

In many ways, your Friends in Facebook will be analogous to your friends in the real world. But the ability to sustain friendships that transcend geographic distance using an excellent and easy-to-use communication platform is an advantage Facebook has over the real world.

Facebook will become valuable to you as you connect with your Friends. Although you must consider your own approach to the quality versus quantity question, in general, the more of your actual friends you have as Friends, the better your Facebook experience will be. If you are starting out in Facebook or have only a small number of Friends, adding more Friends will let you see how Facebook works. If you already have Friends, you probably want to add more of your real-world friends into your Facebook world. In this Lesson, you will learn the basic methods of friending.

Finding Friends

There are several ways to find and connect with other people on Facebook. We want to highlight four of the most common.

First, if you're new to Facebook, the easiest way is to click on **Find Friends** in the blue Facebook navigation bar at the top of the page between your name and **Home**. Eventually, when you have been on Facebook for awhile, this link will disappear.

Second, you can find Friends by using the left-hand side of the blue navigation bar at the top of the page. Click on the **Friends icon** to the right of Facebook and choose **Find Friends** at the far right of the drop-down menu that appears (see Figure 5.1).

Figure 5.1: Find Friends—Navigation Bar

Third, you can find Friends by using their names as search terms in the **Search** box at the top of any page or by watching the People You May Know suggestions that Facebook gives you on the right side of the Home Page (see Figure 5.2).

Fourth, you can use the Find Friends area at the bottom of the FAVORITES section on the left navigation bar (see Figure 5.2) of your Home Page/News Feed.

The **Find Friends** link will bring you to the Find Friends screen (see Figure 5.3). There you will see any Friend Requests that others have sent you as well as a list of e-mail and other programs that you can connect with Facebook to upload your contacts.

Figure 5.2: Facebook Home Page

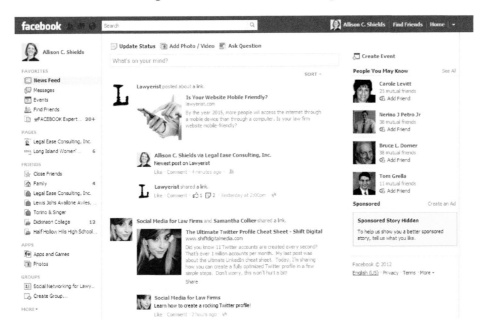

Uploading Your Contacts from Other Services

If you choose one of the ready-made options by clicking on the **Find Friends** link next to it, Facebook will walk you through uploading those contacts and will search through and show you the Friend Selector, which identifies those contacts who are already on Facebook. If you select the **Select All** button at the top, any other action you take will be applied to every one of those contacts. We don't recommend that you do so because Facebook penalizes you if you send numerous Friend requests that are ignored or rejected. Instead, choose individuals separately by checking the box next to their name and click on **Add as Friends** to send them Friend requests. Otherwise, click **Skip** and no invitations will be sent. Clicking Skip will not send any invitations, but your contacts will remain uploaded here for you to search and invite later.

Figure 5.3: Find Friends

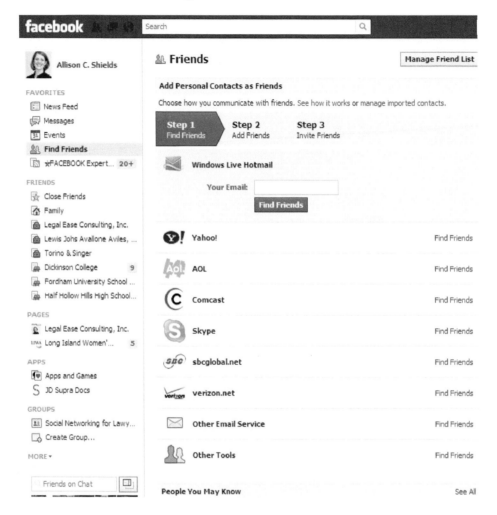

Next, Facebook will show you the contacts that do not have a match on Facebook. You can invite those friends to join Facebook and become your Friend by clicking the **radio button** next to either "invite all Friends" or "invite some Friends" and choose those to whom you would like to send invitations. Otherwise, click **Skip** again.

Other Ways to Find Friends

Under **Other E-mail Service** on the Find Friends page (see Figure 5.3) you will see **Other Tools**. Clicking on that will show an expanded menu of options, including uploading a contact file (from a local file e-mail program such as Outlook), inviting friends by e-mail, and inviting colleagues and classmates from the employers and educational institutions listed in your Profile.

Below Other Tools, Facebook will give you some suggestions under the People You May Know heading (see Figure 5.2). These suggestions are usually based on mutual Facebook Friends. To see more suggestions, click on **Show More** at the bottom of the list. To send a Friend request to any of these individuals, simply click on the **+1 Add Friend** button.

Searching for Friends

If you already know the name of someone you would like to find or Friend on Facebook, you can also simply type his or her name into the Search box in the blue navigation bar at the top of any Facebook page. From the list of results you can click on the **+1 Add as Friend** button next to the result you are seeking. This will send a Friend request.

Alternatively, you can click on the person's name in the search results to go to his or her Timeline to make sure this is the person for whom you were looking. Once you arrive at the Timeline, you may see a number of options under the cover photo on the right, depending on their settings (see Figure 5.4).

If you click on **+1Add Friend**, in addition to sending a Friend request, you also have the option to add the individual to any of your Friend Lists. We discuss Friend Lists in Lesson 6. Facebook will also

Figure 5.4: Timeline Friending Options

automatically subscribe you to receive their public updates in your News Feed. You may also have an option to send the individual a **Message** if you are not yet ready to send a Friend Request (we cover Messages and Subscriptions in more detail in Lesson 8).

Once you have sent a Friend Request, the Friend button will read Friend Request Sent. You can also choose the kind of Updates you would like to receive from this individual. Options include viewing only posts but not photos, receiving only important updates, and receiving all updates. Facebook will notify you that your request has been accepted. Remember the bilateral nature of Friending. If your Request is not accepted, you will not be a Friend of the person to whom you sent the Request. In that case, you might want to follow-up to remind the person to accept your Request.

Using the Manage Friends Feature

You can also find Friends by going to your Manage Friends page (from your **Timeline**, click on the **Find Friends** tab and then **Manage Friends**) and clicking on the **+Find Friends** link on the top right. That will bring you to Find Friends from Different Parts of Your Life. Here you'll see the now-familiar "People You May Know" suggestions, but in addition, along the left, Facebook will give you options to help you narrow your search by location, employer, mutual friend, or educational institution. This tool is great for class reunions, connecting with others at your firm or a former firm, and similar activities. Note that this is the same page to which Facebook will direct you with the Find Friends link in the navigation bar when you are new to Facebook (see Figure 5.5).

Figure 5.5: Find Friends from Different Parts of Your Life

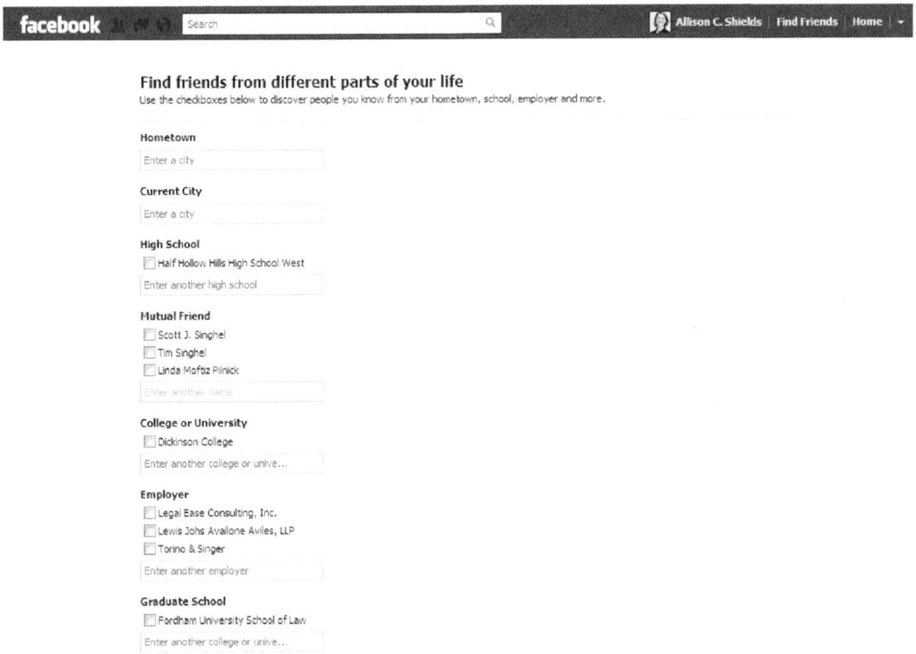

Confirming Friends

When someone sends you a Friend request, you'll be notified by a red bubble on top of the Friends icon in the blue Facebook status bar. Clicking on the icon will bring you to your Friend requests page. Here you will see the photo and name of the person requesting to be your Friend, and Facebook will tell you whether you have mutual friends and who those mutual friends are (click on **# other mutual friends** to see who they are). To confirm the request, click **Confirm**.

If someone sends you a Friend request and you are not sure whether you want to be Friends, you can simply click the **Not Now** link. This will hide the request but keep it in your queue, and you can confirm at any time later. If you change your mind later, click the **See Hidden Requests** link below your Friend Requests to see all of those invitations to which you didn't respond earlier.

As we discuss in Lesson 8, if you don't confirm, the individual can still "subscribe" to your Public Updates if you allow Subscriptions, but otherwise the person will not have the same access to your information as your Friends do.

If you receive a Friend request from someone you do not recognize, you may also choose to send them a private Message if they have Messages enabled to confirm that they are who you think they are. We'll discuss Messages in more detail in Lesson 8.

You can also accept a pending Friend request by visiting the **Timeline** of the requester. There, instead of the Add Friend button beneath his or her cover photo, you'll see a button that reads, **Respond to Friend Request**. Clicking on the button will confirm that you are Friends. But if you're still not sure about accepting, you can also click the **Message** button to send a private message without being Friends. We cover Messages in more depth in Lesson 8.

Friending Strategy

Give some thought to the people with whom you would like to be connected. People often judge you by the company you keep, and that means being judged by who you are publicly Friends with on Facebook.

Also keep in mind the privacy and security concerns that go along with Friending on Facebook. Your Friends can see your Updates and some of your personal information as well as *share your personal information with others* on Facebook. That means your Friends may be able to share your personal information with *their Friends,* as well as with games or apps your Friends use on Facebook. This will depend upon both your privacy settings and their privacy settings, as we discussed in detail in Lesson 2.

So be wise and restrict your Facebook Friends to people you actually know. If you want to simply keep up with others, Subscribe to their Updates instead, as we discuss in Lesson 8. If you want to make your Updates available to people who are not your Friends, make them public or enable Subscriptions so others can subscribe to your Updates without the need to be Friends.

In real life, most of us have different kinds of friends: acquaintances, the parents of our children's friends, our inner circle of friends, our work colleagues, neighbors, and so on. Facebook provides you with tools to separate the information you share with (and receive from) these different levels of Friends.

Don't forget that, if you are using Facebook as a professional networking tool, you'll want to take that into consideration in your Friending strategy. Put on your marketing thinking cap and identify your target audience, which includes your potential clients *and* potential referral sources.

Default Friend Settings

Once you have confirmed a Friend on Facebook (or they have confirmed you), if you do nothing else, Facebook will automatically default those people to a general Friend category. You will be listed as Friends on each other's Timelines. Your Friends can usually see posts and information on your Timeline, and they will also see your new posts on their News Feed. Similarly, you will be able to see their posts on their Timeline, and you will receive their Updates in your News Feed.

Customizing Friend Settings

You don't need to stick with Facebook's default Friend settings—you can customize both what your different Friends see on your Timeline (and which posts or Updates they can see in their News Feed), as well as how much of your Friends' posts and Updates you see in your News Feed.

Managing Friends

You can manage your Friend lists from the navigation bar on your Home page. Click on the **Find Friends** in the list on the left and then click on the **Manage Friends List** link at the upper right. That will take you to a page with all of your Friends' names and photos. From here, you can click on **Edit** and edit who sees your Friend list on your Timeline.

Facebook also allows you to block specific people. When you block someone, you will be invisible to them (and they will be invisible to you) on Facebook; you won't be able to see one another's Profiles or Timelines, send Friend requests, or view comments each other makes on mutual Friends' Timelines.

The most powerful way to manage Friends is to sort them into Friend Lists, which are groupings of related Friends. Now that you have added some Friends, you will be ready to explore Friend Lists, and that is the topic for Lesson 6.

Organizing Friends with Friend Lists

As in the real world, Friends are essential to making Facebook useful and valuable. In Lesson 5, we showed you how to add Friends. As your number of Friends start to grow, you may have questions about managing them, such as:

- Does the Update you post for your professional colleagues make any sense to your siblings, in-laws, or aunts and uncles, and vice versa?
- Should all of your Friends see your vacation and family photos?
- Should all of your Friends see your jokes, political rants, and sports commentary?
- Should you have Friended co-workers, your boss, your competitors, your clients, expert witnesses, judges, or jurors?

Fortunately, Facebook has offered a feature called Friend Lists to help you sort and manage your Friends into handy personalized collections. Although the Friend List feature has been around for quite some time, surprisingly few people know that much about it. If you are familiar with the GooglePlus social media platform, Friend Lists is analogous to the GooglePlus Circles feature.

Friend Lists are especially attractive to lawyers because they can help you separate your personal and professional lives and send Friends appropriate information.

There are two types of Friend Lists: automatic and manual. The automatic lists are called Smart Lists and they are created based on your interactions and other shared characteristics. You can also manually create your own Friend Lists using whatever criteria you want.

Facebook gives you a lot of flexibility in setting up Friend Lists. A Friend List can currently have up to 1,500 members, and each of your Friends can be on multiple Friend Lists. Currently, you can create as many as 100 Friend Lists.

Friend Lists have several benefits. One is that you can target your postings appropriately. For example, you can post family reunion photos to your Family list and not to your Legal Business Referrers list. Another is that you can use a Friend List to reach a certain group of people quickly and easily. For example, you can send an event invitation to the Inventor Clients, Book Discussion Club, or Poker Night Friend List. You can also use Friend Lists in connection with privacy settings to control information flow and access. Best of all, the existence and names of Friend Lists currently cannot be seen by others (unless they happen to be looking over your shoulder).

Smart Lists

Facebook automatically creates Smart Lists for you, and they include Family, Close Friends, Acquaintances, High School, College, and Workplace. It's worth noting that the Acquaintances Smart List can be used in connection with a privacy setting option called Friends Except Acquaintances, which allows you to share certain information with only your closest friends.

Facebook draws from your information and connections and the information of your Friends in fairly obvious ways. For example, if your Profile includes the college you attended, Facebook will create a Smart List for your Friends who went to the same college. You can find your Smart Lists in the left column of your Facebook Home page under the FRIENDS heading (see Figure 6.1).

Figure 6.1: Home Page Showing Friend Lists

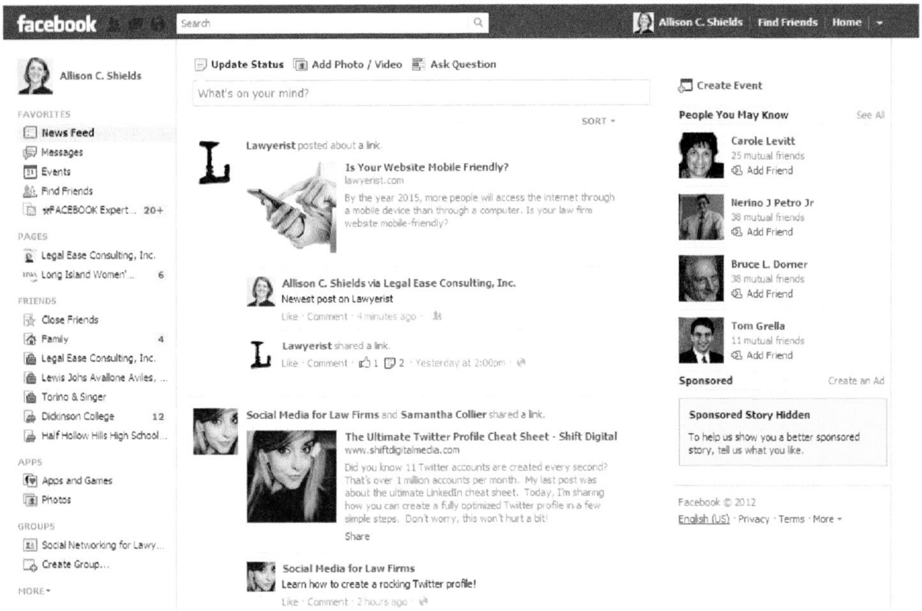

The Lists will show you a small number indicating the number of Friends on the list. If you hover your mouse pointer just to the right of the FRIENDS heading, you'll see a **MORE** button. Click on that and you'll see all of your lists (see Figure 6.2).

Most of the time, Facebook does a good job creating Smart Lists, but you might want to adjust or edit the lists. For example, you might want to limit "Family" to a short list of immediate family members. That's easy to do.

Figure 6.2: Lists

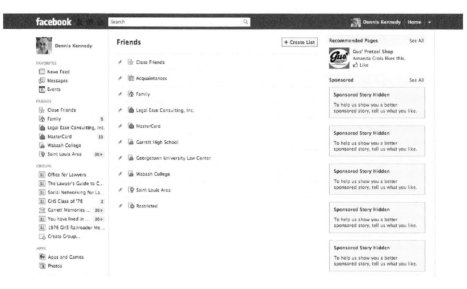

Click on the **Smart List** you want to edit. You'll see who is on the list, suggestions for additions to the list, and updates from people on the lists.

At the top of the right column, you will also see a **Manage List** button. Click on it and you can rename, edit, and control what displays on the list. As an aside, if you limit the Family Smart List to your immediate family, you will have a handy way to see everything your children post on Facebook (assuming they let you Friend them or see what they post, of course).

Manual Friend Lists

Smart Lists can help you get started with Friend Lists, but you might have some specific groups in mind—clients, colleagues, people you met at a conference, etc. In many cases, you'll want to want to create your own Friend List.

It will be an easy and familiar process. On the **Home** page, go to the **FRIENDS** category in the list in the left column. Hover your mouse pointer over FRIENDS until you see the **MORE** button and then click on it. You'll again be at your list of Friend Lists (see Figure 6.2).

At the top right of the middle column, you'll see a **+ Create List button.** Click on it and a Create New List pop-up menu appears (see Figure 6.3).

Figure 6.3: Create New List Pop-Up

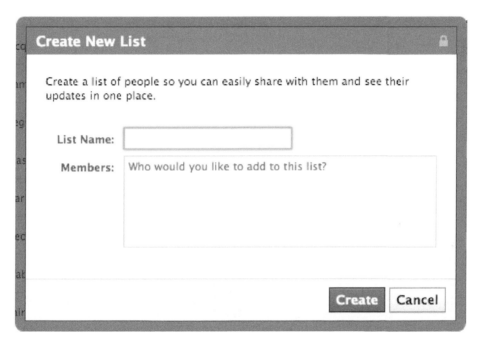

There's a space to type in the name of your list and a box into which you add the Friends you want to add to your list. As you start to type their names into the box, their full names will appear on a drop-down menu and you can just click on the Friend rather than typing the entire name. Add the Friends you want and click the **Create**

button. You now have a new Friend List. It appears as a choice anywhere using Friend Lists is available in Facebook.

You can edit manually created Friend Lists just as you can Smart Lists using the method we discussed previously. You can also add Friends to a Friend List by going to your lists of all Friends. Find the Friend you want to add to a Friend List and simply hover your mouse pointer over the Friend's picture until the pop-up appears with more information about the Friend. In the bottom-right corner of the pop-up, you'll see a button that reads **Friend**. Click on this button and you'll find a number of options relating to lists. Make the appropriate selections and you are all set.

Friend Lists can be very useful in managing communications and access through Facebook. It should be obvious how good use of Friend Lists can help you separate the personal from the professional and keep the appropriate tone and appearance in Facebook that you want for each type of Friend.

We recommend starting with a few basic Friend Lists that make sense for you and seeing how they work. If they are helpful to you, build a few more lists. But resist the urge to spend a weekend organizing all of your Friends into dozens of Friend Lists. Keep it simple. If you find yourself with lists like Close Friends, Really Close Friends, Really Really Close Friends, and Super Close Friends, you've probably gone too far. Think in practical terms and useful lists, such as Estate Planning Referrers, Bar Committee, School Parents, Soccer Team, and the like.

Now it's time to move to the third essential building block of Facebook—participation. In Lesson 7, you'll learn about Status Updates, Likes, Comments, and Sharing.

Participating by Updates, Comments, Likes, and Sharing

Participation is the third essential component of Facebook. In the next two Lessons, we cover many of the forms of participation in Facebook. In this Lesson, we focus on the first set of tools: Updates, Comments, Likes, and Sharing. The other participation tools will be covered in Lesson 8.

As an individual Facebook user, you can interact with other individuals or with Pages created by businesses or organizations. The amount of content others post on Facebook that you can access depends first on whether you are Friends with them. However, take note: Pages are considered public by Facebook, which means all posts on Pages, whether by Subscribers to the Page or by the Page Administrator(s), are public, as we noted in Lesson 4. By contrast, on your individual account, you have the ability to determine who can see your information and Updates, as discussed in Lesson 2 and later in this Lesson.

Participation on Facebook is more personal and intimate than participation on LinkedIn, where it's all business with a focus on professional discussions, business connections, and career advancement. Although there is a fair amount of business discussion on Facebook (depending upon who your Friends are), participation on Facebook is more about what goes on in people's personal lives—what they do every day, their daily struggles and successes, and what they find humorous or interesting.

For better or worse, you get to know people on a much more human level on Facebook than on LinkedIn. Updates on LinkedIn are only seen in e-mail notifications or on your LinkedIn Homepage, which is not where most people spend their time on LinkedIn. In contrast, your Facebook Updates are much more visible to your Friends and subscribers—and to their Friends and subscribers. Most Facebook users spend their time in their News Feed, and they are more likely to see your Updates because the News Feed occupies the primary real estate on their Home page. They will also see when you Like or Comment on a post here.

Updates

Updates are posts on Facebook that can be seen by different audiences, depending on who you want to see them (the general public, just Friends, and so on). If you are familiar with Twitter, Updates are similar to tweets, although without Twitter's 140-character limitation. Updates can be news, comments, thoughts, observations, or whatever you want. They can include links, photos, and videos. In the simplest terms, think of Updates as your current answer to the question, "What's on your mind?"

Status Updates—How To

Status Updates, which Facebook sometimes refers to as "stories," contain content you want to share with Friends, Subscribers, or the Public. Think of your Updates as the beginning of a conversation; other people can Like or comment on your Updates and continue the conversation.

Create Updates by clicking in the **Status Update** box on either your Timeline (see Figure 7.1) or at the top of your Home page/News Feed

Figure 7.1: Timeline Status Update Box

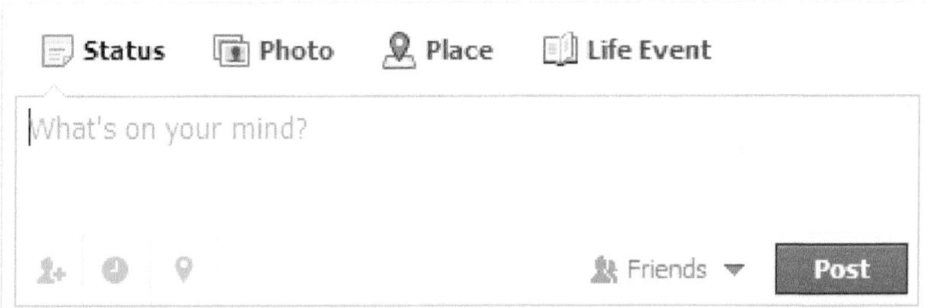

(see Figure 7.2). As you can see, these two Status Update boxes are slightly different, but you can provide updates from either location.

The buttons at the top of the Status Update box let you choose what type of Update you are posting. For example, by clicking the **Place** button (see Figure 7.1) you can check in and tell your Friends where you are. Clicking on the **Life Event** button creates a special Timeline post related to a significant event. (We'll discuss Life Events in more detail later in this Lesson.) Clicking on **Photo** brings up a dialog box to help you upload photographs. From your Home page/News Feed, you can also choose the **Ask Question** option to create a poll (see Figure 7.2).

Figure 7.2: Home Page Status Update Box

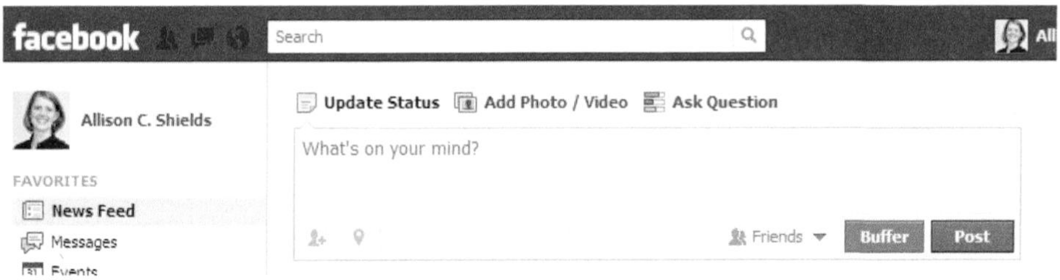

Some readers may remember that Facebook used to include a separate button on the Status Updates box to allow you to share a link. That link button no longer exists, but you can still share links by typing or pasting the URL directly into your Update.

When you click in the **Status Update** box from your **Timeline**, you'll see some additional icons appear at the bottom of the box. The **Friends icon** to the left (the person with the + sign) allows you to tag a post indicating who is with you when you're posting the Update. The **clock icon** lets you date your post; if you're posting a story about something in the past, this will place your story at the correct time on your Timeline (Note: this option is currently not available when posting from your Home page/News Feed). The **Place icon** (the one that looks like a map pin) tags your post with a location.

On the bottom right of the **Status Update** box is a **Friends** button, and next to it is a **down arrow** that you can click to change the audience for your post. Click **Post** when you've completed your entry and it will be published to your Timeline and will be seen on your Friends' News Feeds.

Status Updates: What to Share

What you share in your Updates depends on how you use Facebook and how personal you want to be. Many people post personal likes and dislikes, information about current activities, photos from vacations or restaurant meals, links to topical or humorous articles or blog posts, videos, and other aspects of daily life. On a professional note, you can post industry news, tips, articles, and links of interest. Post links to your content on your blog, newsletter, or website, but be sure to share others' content that your audience might find interesting as well, and provide your own commentary so your posts are not purely self-promotional. You might consider Updates as a form of microblogging.

Although you can use any style or approach you want in Updates, posting questions in your Updates encourages engagement, and offering help (where ethical and appropriate) can give Friends and Subscribers a better idea about what you do. Provide value, but remember that entertainment value also counts on Facebook. Speak as if you are speaking directly to individual Friends to make your stories sound more personal and increase interaction.

Placing Updates in the Correct Location on the Timeline

One of the features of the new Facebook Timeline (as opposed to the old Wall format) is that when you upload information or photographs, they are now placed chronologically instead of automatically at the top of the page. Originally, you could not enter information that occurred prior to the date you joined Facebook, and entries appeared chronologically based on the date you posted them. Now Facebook allows you to tell the whole story of your life and put photographs and content (called "stories") where they belong on your Timeline.

For example, if you join Facebook now, but you would like to share photographs from (or stories about) college, law school, your first home, and so on, you can attach a date when you upload the photographs or create those entries, and Facebook will place the entry chronologically on your Timeline. So if you graduated from law school in 1993 and you identify your law school graduation pictures as from 1993, they will appear under 1993 in your Timeline. However, the story about you posting the photos will appear in the News Feed when you post them so your Friends see the story and photos now.

Tagging

You can also "tag" people in your posts, especially when you are linking to their content or praising them. Tagging links people, Pages, or places to your post. When you tag someone else in a post, your Update will appear in tht person's Timeline (but only if the person is your Friend). Your Friend will be notified that they have been tagged. Tagging is a good way to "tip your hat" to a Friend that you have mentioned them, but you may also want to consider that person's privacy when tagging them (or their children) in a photo or post.

To tag someone by name, type the @ **symbol** and his or her name in an Update or comment. To tag a photo, hover your mouse over the photo and click **Tag Photo**. Then click on the person in the photograph and enter his or her name. Once the photo is tagged, others viewing the photo can hover over the photo to see the names of the people pictured. See Lesson 2 for Privacy settings related to tagging and how you can keep the right to approve the display of tagged items.

Checking In

Checking in tells Friends on Facebook where you are. It is done through the Places feature on your smartphone or other mobile device. When you tap **Check In**, your device GPS will bring up a list of nearby places; choose where you are (or enter the name if it doesn't appear in the list) and Facebook will create a story on your Timeline to show Friends where you are. You can add a description of what you are doing or tag Friends who are with you. The story on your Timeline will include a map and will say something like, "Allison Shields was with Dennis Kennedy at the ABA TECHSHOW." The story may also appear in Friends' News Feeds, and if you tag others when you check in, it will appear in the tagged individuals' Timelines as well. Be aware of privacy and security issues and settings when using this feature.

Starring Stories on the Timeline

When you hover over a story in your Timeline, two icons appear: one is the pencil icon that gives you editing options, and the other is the star. Click on the **star** to highlight posts you think are important. The post expands to widescreen—the full width of your Timeline. Over time, Timeline posts will "collapse" and become hidden, but starred stories always stay on your Timeline.

Life Events

A Life Event is a significant story about your life and might include the birth of a child, a new job, graduating from law school, or becoming a partner in your firm. Life Events are automatically starred on your Timeline. The default audience is Public, but you can adjust the audience as you choose. When you create a Life Event, you can also tag others or choose a date to place so that it is placed chronologically on your Timeline.

Who Sees What You Share on Facebook

With one important exception, you control who sees your Updates and other information you share on Facebook. We discussed those privacy settings in detail in Lesson 2. For example, if you restrict the viewing of your Updates to Friends but enable Subscriptions, when you post an Update you designate as Public, both Friends and Subscribers who are not your Friends will be able to see what you share; it will appear in the News Feeds of each. The exception is that, if your Friends Share your Update, *their* Friends will also see the Update because sharing puts the update on your Friend's Timeline. There is also an exception to the exception: if you have excluded an individual from being able to see your Update, that person will still not be able to see the Update if someone else Shares it. Updates posted to businesses' Pages appear in the News Feed of people who Like the Page.

Restricting the Audience for Updates or Posts

As discussed above, when you create an Update, you can restrict who sees it on your Timeline. Look for the **Post** link and click the **down arrow** next to it to designate the audience. But you can also change the audience for a post later (or hide it from your Timeline completely) by finding the story in your Timeline and clicking on the **audience icon** and changing it there.

Story Visibility Over Time

Unless you hide a post from your Timeline, it will be available, but over time, as you add more things to your Timeline, some of your stories will collapse behind grey dots on your Timeline. Hover your mouse pointer over these dots to view hidden posts, or click **Resize** to move the post back onto the visible Timeline.

Liking, Commenting, and Sharing

In addition to writing your own posts, you can interact on Facebook by Commenting, Liking, and Sharing the posts created by others. Think of each of these as ways to continue the conversation your Friends started with their posts or photos. We talked a bit about Liking in Lesson 3 when we discussed how Likes appear in your Profile, but in addition to liking things you are interested in, such as movies and music, Likes can be a way of interacting on Facebook.

The Like, Comment, and Share links appear at the bottom of posts in a Timeline (as seen in Figure 7.3) or at the bottom of posts in your News Feed.

Liking

When you Like an Update, Page, Photo, Post, or Comment, or when you click a Like button on another website, you are interacting with the person who posted that content and showing your support without having to write a separate message. Your Like will appear on your Timeline, and it can be seen by anyone who was able to see the original post on which you commented. It may also appear in News Feeds.

Figure 7.3: Liking, Commenting, and Sharing

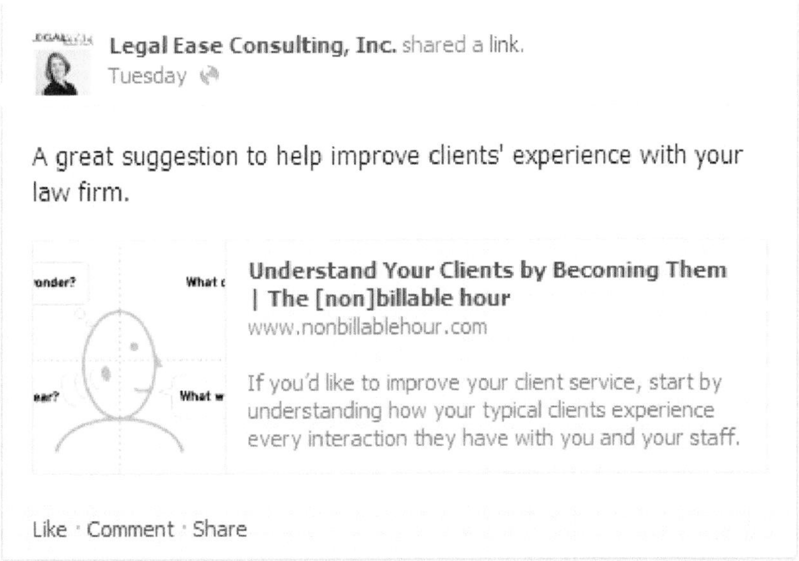

Legal Ease Consulting, Inc. shared a link.
Tuesday

A great suggestion to help improve clients' experience with your law firm.

Understand Your Clients by Becoming Them | The [non]billable hour
www.nonbillablehour.com

If you'd like to improve your client service, start by understanding how your typical clients experience every interaction they have with you and your staff.

Like · Comment · Share

If you Like a Page, your name will be listed as someone who Liked the Page, and you may receive updates from the Page in your News Feed. (The only way to receive Page Updates is by Liking the Page.)

Commenting

Commenting on a post or photograph in Facebook is just what it sounds like: adding your comments to others' posts, photographs, or other content on Facebook. Comments are a higher level of involvement than a simple Like. Just as with Likes, when you comment on someone else's post, your Comment can be seen not only by that person, but also by whoever can see that post on their Timeline. Comments have the same privacy settings as the original post of your Friend. As a result, when commenting on others' status updates, photos, etc., keep in mind that your comment may be public and not restricted to your Friends.

Sharing

The Share feature may be one of the most useful for creating relationships. Not only does the **Share** button allow you to share important or interesting content with your Friends and those in your various lists, but it also extends your relationship with the person whose content you share. When others share your content, it reaches a larger audience. When Friends share your content or post on their Timeline, their Friends see it, giving you additional exposure (or, if you are not careful, unexpected exposure). In addition to sharing content from your own Timeline and News Feed, you can share from other locations in Facebook and around the web.

To re-share something someone else has shared on Facebook, click on the "Share" link you see at the bottom of the story. When you do, a pop-up window will appear with options for sharing the link, photo, or other content and with whom (see Figure 7.4). When you click on the **Share** link, instead of just commenting on the post, photo, or link in your Friend's Timeline, you are sharing that content with your own Friends and subscribers on *your* Timeline (or Page). When your Friends share your content, they also share it with *their* Friends.

Use the **down arrows** to bring up the drop-down menus to control where you share the link (options include on your own Timeline or your Page's Timeline, in a private Message, and in a Group) and with whom you share: Public, Friends, and so on. You can also write your own message to accompany the link or photo and choose whether to display a thumbnail image along with the link.

Figure 7.4: Share This Link

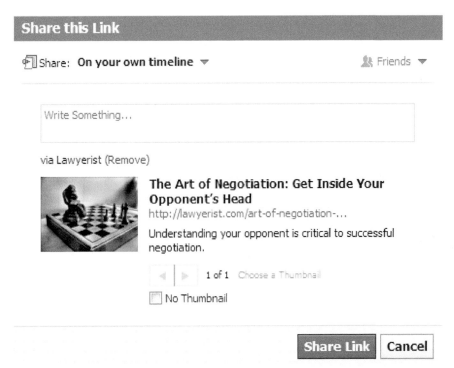

Facebook is a social network. Expand your network through observing your Friends' friends and what they share or care about. See what they post and how they comment. From there, you can see their Timelines and posts and interact with them directly.

Updates, Likes, Comments, and Shares are not the only participation tools on Facebook. In the next Lesson, we cover some powerful communication and interaction tools built into Facebook.

Participation Through Messages, Groups, and Subscriptions

Perhaps the most important aspect of Facebook is how it increasingly serves as a platform for having communications and conversations with the people we care about even though we are separated by geographic or other distances. These can take the form of one-to-one communications, both asynchronous (as in e-mail) and real-time (as in texting). You can also have group conversations of various kinds. And you can simply see the Updates of others without the need to Friend them by using subscription tools.

To network effectively, you must nurture your relationships. As in real-world networking activities, simply joining Facebook is not enough. Facebook's real value grows from building genuine relationships with the other people who are in your target audience, whether that target audience is personal (friends and family) or professional (clients, referral sources, or strategic alliances).

Facebook's communication tools give you several easy and effective ways to communicate and have conversations with your Friends so that you can keep in touch and interact with them, and build vibrant networks. If Updates and the other tools we discussed in Lesson 7 are ways to help you stay top of mind with your Friends, the tools discussed in this Lesson enable you to have direct interaction and conversations with Friends and others.

Messages and Chat

The Facebook communication tool you will probably use most often is Messages. You can think of Messages as Facebook's internal e-mail system, even though Messages are both simpler and more complex than that description might suggest.

There are two easy ways access Messages on your Home page: a link to **Messages** in the left column and also a small **messages icon** (two square speech balloons) on the left side of the top blue navigation bar (see Figure 8.1).

Figure 8.1: Home Page

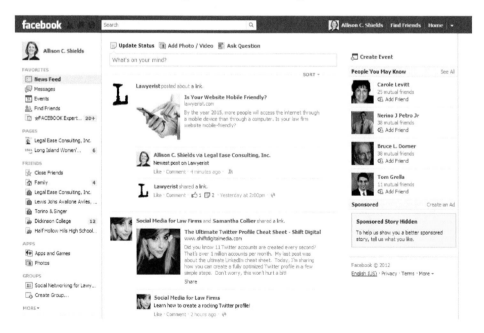

Let's start with the Messages icon in the top navigation bar. If you have unread messages, the icon will have a red bubble with the number of waiting messages. Whether or not you have any messages, click on the icon and you'll see your Messages inbox as a drop-down (see Figure 8.2).

Figure 8.2: Messages Inbox

The drop-down shows a few of your recent messages and gives you a link to show more messages at the bottom. In the top right-hand corner of the drop-down is a link to **Create New Message**. When you click on that, you'll see a pop-up to create a Message (see Figure 8.3).

The pop-up has a "To:" box for your recipient, a box for writing your Message, and a few icons. Select your recipient by name. (You do not need to know his or her e-mail address.) Starting to type in a name activates the auto-complete feature, and you'll soon see the name you want. Click on the name to add the person as a recipient. You can also

Figure 8.3: Create Message Pop-Up

add other recipients or send to Friend Lists or Groups by typing in a Friend List or Group name.

Then type your message into the Message box. As a practical matter, you can type as much as you want into the Message, much like in a regular e-mail application. It's worth noting that Messages are, by their nature, private, like regular e-mail, although you'll want to read Facebook's privacy policy to get a better understanding of what that might mean. Of course, like e-mail, nothing prevents someone from forwarding your Message, copying and pasting your message and sending it to someone else, or simply telling someone in person what you said.

The icons at the bottom of the pop-up show how powerful and versatile the Facebook messaging platform is. You can attach files, take a picture or video to send, or send the Message to a mobile phone.

Once you are ready, click **Send** and your Message will be delivered to your recipient's Message inbox in Facebook. Messages stay within the Facebook system and do not go to external e-mail addresses, although you might set up e-mail notifications to alert you that you have received a Message.

Note that, if you decide to access your Messages through the Messages link in the left column of your Home page, the process is similar. It's a matter of which method you prefer.

Now go to the left column and click on **Messages** and two things happen. Your Messages inbox appears to the right and a small link to Other appears below Messages in the left column (see Figure 8.2). The Other link takes you to a separate inbox for Messages from sources other than Friends (e.g., invitations to events). Facebook uses the main inbox for the Messages it has decided are most important—those from your Friends.

The main Messages inbox will remind you of the inbox in your regular e-mail application, but you'll see your received messages and your sent messages all in one place as ongoing conversations. Above the list of Messages, you'll find a box labeled **+ New Message**. Click on it and you'll see the same Message creation pop-up we discussed above. You'll also see a Search box that lets you search your Messages.

Each Message shows the picture of the Friend who sent it and a short excerpt from the beginning of the Message. This excerpt takes the place of the traditional e-mail subject line. The idea is that most Messages to Friends will be short and to the point and that subject lines are unnecessary. To the right are icons for marking the Message as read and for archiving the Message (to remove it from your active inbox).

Click on the Message to read it and activate messaging tools (see Figure 8.4). The first thing you will notice is that you see the current Message as well as the whole thread of Messages if you have been messaging this Friend. If you want to reply, there is a **Reply** box at the bottom that works like the Create Message pop-up we have discussed previously. Write your reply and click on **Send** to send it. There's also a checkbox for enabling **Quick Replies**—a way to send messages simply by pressing the Enter key on your keyboard.

Figure 8.4: Message Page

In the right column of the Message page, Facebook suggests potential Friends for you. At the top, you'll find a **Search** box to search the conversation with this Friend and a button called **Actions** with a small **gear icon** and an **inverted triangle.** When you see a gear and/or an inverted triangle on Facebook, you know that there will be a drop-down menu with context-relevant tools and options similar to what you see when you right-click with your mouse in almost all programs today. That's the case here, too.

Click on the **Actions** button to see the list of options. You can mark the message as unread, forward it, archive it, move it out of your main inbox to the Other inbox, or delete it. You can also report it to Facebook as spam or as violating Facebook's terms of use.

Chat

If the other person is currently online, you can even move to a real-time chat session. Click on the **Open in Chat** option in the Actions drop-down menu to see a chat pop-up (see Figure 8.5).

Figure 8.5: Chat Pop-Up

In the chat pop-up, you'll see the Message thread and a small box at the bottom below the last message from the Friend to type in an instant message for chat purposes. You need to be "online" in Facebook to chat. At the top of the pop-up, you'll see a **gear icon** for options. Click on it and you can choose to **go online** and see other chat options. If you go online, your Friends will see that you are online on their Home page. Next to the gear icon is an **icon for video calls** that you might use if the recipient is online and has activated that service for you. Facebook video chat gives you a simple way to do videoconferencing. You can even add other people to the chat. It's important to know that, when you add someone, they can see the discussion that occurred before they joined, so be careful.

Group Messages

Messages to groups of people work in much the same way as individual Messages. You create (or receive) a Message with multiple recipients.

Each reply then works like a "reply to all" e-mail where all the recipients see your reply. Keep that in mind. You cannot individually message someone from a Group Message. You can add people to a Group Message, but remember that they can then see the prior conversation.

If you prefer Chat (instant messaging) to regular Messaging, you will see a small Chat icon at the bottom right of every screen. Clicking on the icon will give you the option to go online. Additional options, found by clicking the gear icon, include Advanced Settings, which allow you to choose which Friends can see that you are online. Once you are online, you can see how many and which of your Friends are online so you can initiate a chat session with them. There is also a search box. You can hide the sidebar with the list of your Friends who are online. When you do so, if you remain online, the Chat icon will indicate how many of your Friends are online.

Groups

In the real world, we deal with people in groups based on location, projects, interests, history, and the like. Facebook's Groups feature allows you to join existing Groups or create your own. Lawyers may find Groups an especially attractive tool for networking, creating communities of common interest, and for some marketing purposes.

Joining Groups

You can use Facebook's search tool to find Groups that interest you. You might learn about Groups from Friends, or you might receive invitations to join Groups. A great example of a Group that many people join is a Group for their high school reunion. Lawyers might also find and join Groups related to practice areas, bar activities, or specific legal issues. Once you find a Group, you'll see a button to make a request to join.

For purposes of this Lesson, we're going to assume that you've already joined a few Groups. If not, search for the Social Networking for Lawyers Group we've created for this book and join it so you can better follow the discussion below.

Go to your Home page. In the left column, you'll see a GROUPS heading with some of your Groups listed below it. Click on the **GROUPS** link and you'll see a list of all your Groups (see Figure 8.6).

Figure 8.6: Groups Page

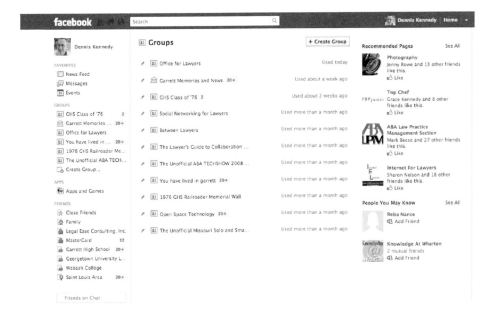

On the page, you'll see a **Create Groups** button at the top that we'll discuss later. The listing of your Groups includes a small blue box with the number of your new and unread postings and a useful notation of when the last activity in the Group occurred. Click on a **Group** and you'll see the home page for the Group (see Figure 8.7).

Group Home Pages look like your Home Page or Timeline, so the navigation and features should seem familiar. The main feature is the

Figure 8.7: Social Networking for Lawyers Group Page

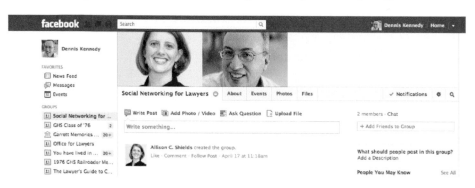

center column with a News Feed of all the Updates from Group members and the Comments to those Updates. This is where the Group conversation happens.

Across the top are a number of features. The **About** button tells you whether the Group is Open, Closed, or Secret. Given that everyone in the Group can see what you post to the Group, it is vital to know what type of Group you are joining.

- **Open Groups.** Anyone can join and no approval is necessary. Anyone can see members and content. Open Groups make sense for large, public Groups.
- **Closed Groups.** Requires a request to join and administrator approval. Anyone can see the list of members, but only members can see content.
- **Secret Groups.** Almost impossible to find. Essentially, you will need an invitation from the Group owner to join. Only members can see the member list and content.

Knowing the type of Group is essential and must be taken into account when you consider what you post and how you participate. Note that new members can be added after you join so people you might not have expected to be part of the Group could now see content you did not plan for them to see.

Next to the About button, you'll find buttons for **Events, Photos,** and **Files.** You can see what has been posted and create new events, post photos, and create files. To the right is the **gear icon,** which gives you options for Group chat and other tools. You can also add (or suggest) members to the Group. The **magnifying glass icon** is the Groups search tool.

Just above the News Feed is a **Status Updates** box for posting an Update to the Group. You can also post photos and videos, ask a question to the Group to start a discussion, or upload a File.

A class reunion Group or a book discussion Group is a classic example of a Group and will illustrate the potential value and power of a Group. Lawyers might use Groups for discussion of legal issues, connection to lawyers with the same practice area (or different areas if seeking referrals), targeted communication to clients, participation in bar committees, and many other possibilities.

Creating Groups

Groups are very easy to create, but before you create one, consider how much work administering and managing a Group will be. If you decide to create your own Group, go to your Facebook Home page, click on **GROUPS** in the left column (see Figure 8.6 above), and then click on the **Create Group** button. You'll then see a Create Group pop-up (see Figure 8.8).

It's a simple three-step process. Choose a name for your Group. Pick some Friends to invite. Then select the type of Group you want— Open, Closed, or Secret. The default, appropriately, is Closed. Think carefully before choosing an Open or Secret Group. If you have any questions, click on the **Learn More** link at the bottom of the pop-up. Click on the **Create** button and you now have your new Group.

Figure 8.8: Create Group Pop-Up

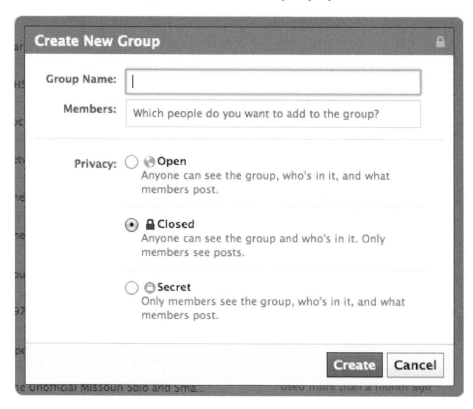

As a Group administrator, you will see something called Edit Group under the options under the gear icon on your Group's page (Figure 8.9).

Here you can control and change the configuration and management of your Group. You can also can remove or ban members from the Group by using the edit functions on the member list or add someone else as an administrator to help you manage your Group.

Unless you create a Secret Group, people will be able to search for and find your Group in Facebook. You will also want to use other outlets (web page, print, blog, and so on) to publicize your Group if you've created it for professional or marketing purposes. You can see

Figure 8.9: Edit Group Page

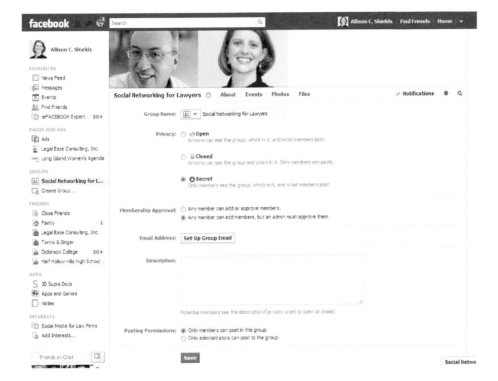

that a Group could function as a mini-website or mini-blog for your practice, an interactive version of your firm's newsletter, or a discussion board for new legal developments.

Subscriptions

The subscription option is used when you want to read the public Updates of a thought leader, famous person, or someone else whom you don't really have any relationship with and doubt would accept your Friend invitation. If that person has the Subscription option enabled on their Page or Profile, you can subscribe to the person's public Updates, much as you might follow someone on Twitter.

Navigate to the person's Timeline to see if the person has enabled the Subscription feature. If so, a Subscribe button is at the top right of the page. Click on that button and you can set what Updates you receive—All, Most, or Only Important—and whether you want Photos, Likes, and other items in addition to Status Updates. If that person posts Updates as Public, they will appear in your News Feed even though you are not Friends.

In a professional setting, enabling the Subscription feature for yourself might be a good way to allow people to access your Facebook content without Friending them. However, if you do this, you will need to think very carefully about what you post to your Facebook account as Public and who will see it. Note that Subscribers will not be able to see Updates and other posted items (e.g., photos) for which you set the Audience as Friends or Custom.

Summing Up

Facebook has a wide variety of powerful and easy-to-use participation and conversation tools that can be used in their simplest form or with depth and richness. The convenience of these tools is one good reason that people who use Facebook tend to stay on Facebook for a significant amount of time each day. Facebook can work as something of an e-mail substitute, an instant-messaging tool, and even as a simple video-conferencing tool through the video-chat features.

The real value for lawyers, however, might well come from Groups and the ways Groups allow you to gather and sustain relevant groups of people in your network. Groups are a good step toward creating a professional or practice-related Facebook presence with an audience of people interested in the subject matter of your Group.

In Lesson 9, we discuss ways to monitor what's happening in your Facebook network and how that can help you with networking in the real world.

Monitoring Your Facebook Network

In many ways, Facebook maps your real-world networks and what you do in them into an Internet format and service. In this Lesson, we discuss something that great real-world networkers do really well—monitor their networks and keep track of what is going on with the people in them. Facebook gives you several ways to keep up with your networks so you can start to create actual communities of common interests and mutual benefit.

We'll cover four effective ways you can monitor your Facebook network: the Facebook Home page, the Timeline, Notifications, and the Facebook mobile app.

Home Page

For purposes of this Lesson, we want to focus on the middle column of your Home page, where you will see the News Feed we discussed in detail in Lesson 7. (Remember you can easily get to your Home page by clicking on **Home** in the top blue navigation bar.)

The News Feed lets you see what is happening in your network of Friends by giving you a running list of your Friends' posts, including Updates, comments on those Updates, and much more. In just a few minutes each day, you can get a good idea of happenings in your network of Friends by scrolling down your News Feed. You will quickly learn what Friends are doing, what they find interesting, and other details of their Facebook lives. You can also easily Like or Comment on these posts directly from the News Feed.

There are currently two ways you can display or sort your News Feed: either showing the most recent posts first (i.e., in reverse chronological order) or allowing Facebook to organize by what it deems to be your Top Stories. At the top of your News Feed, you'll see either SORT: MOST RECENT or SORT: TOP STORIES, with the familiar inverted triangle to the right. Clicking on the **inverted triangle** lets you toggle between views (see Figure 9.1).

Figure 9.1: Home Page with Sorting Options

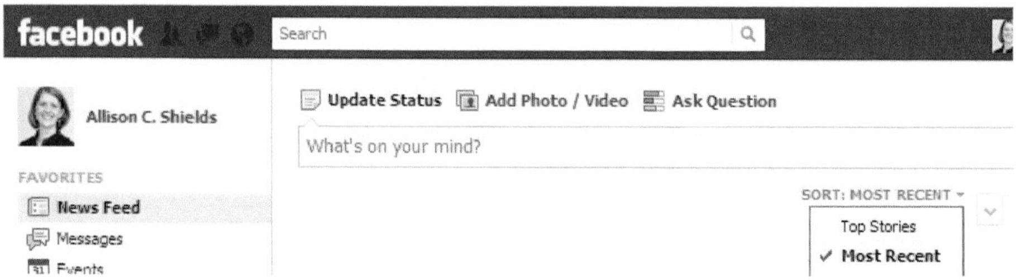

You might experiment to see which sorting method you prefer. In the Top Stories sort, Facebook applies what it knows about your relationships and interactions with Friends to determine which Updates you might find most important and bring them to the top of the News Feed. Obviously, you will be relying on the accuracy of Facebook's algorithms. We prefer the Most Recent search so we can make our own decisions about what is most important.

As you move down the Updates in your New Feeds, you should notice a small box with a small down arrow to the right that becomes visible as you hover your mouse pointer over the Update (see Figure 9.2).

Figure 9.2: Update Detail

Clicking on the **down arrow** gives you a menu of choices for managing Updates from that Friend (see Figure 9.3).

Figure 9.3: Managing Updates Menu

Some of you might find this menu and its options revelatory and alone worth the price of this book. This context menu lets you hide the Update so you can tidy up your News Feed. You can also set whether you get all Updates from the Friend, most Updates, or only important Updates (as determined by Facebook algorithms). These can be useful settings for Friends who post a lot of Updates, especially Friends obsessed by politics, sports, or other issues. It might be a better choice than "unfriending." This context menu also lets you manage subscriptions from the person.

Pay attention here because this menu also helps you when you receive Updates from your Friends through games and apps. These kinds of Updates can be annoying, clutter up your News Feed, and make you doubt the sanity of your game-playing Friends. When you get an Update about a game or app, the context menu gives a choice to **hide all Updates from that game or app.** Click on that and never see a Farmville update from a Friend again. (You're welcome.)

Note also that in the right column on your Home Page, you'll see suggestions of people you might know, upcoming Events, and Friends who are having birthdays.

Timelines

Timelines can also be used to monitor your network. Although your own Timeline focuses on you and your activities, it can also be a handy way to get a sense of what is happening in your network, especially through the Comments on your Updates and Friends' Updates that mention you.

Checking the Timelines of Friends from time to time is also a great way to see in one place everything that they are doing in Facebook. If you are calling someone or meeting them in the real world, a brief visit to his or her Timeline will help you prepare and be perceived as attentive and interested.

Notifications

Using your Home page or Timeline to keep tabs on what's happening in your network of Friends requires that you actually go to the Facebook website. But Facebook also has an elaborate set of ways you can get notifications of what is happening on Facebook, by e-mail or even by text message if you enable that option.

As we discuss in Lesson 2, you can use the inverted triangle on the right of the top blue navigation bar (see Figure 2.1) to reach your Account Settings. Once there, you can find the Notification settings in the left column (see Figure 2.2) and customize your notifications.

There are many notifications you can receive. As we write this book, there are nineteen general Facebook notifications alone that you can set. And that doesn't include notifications from apps, games, and the like. You should work through these and decide the types of events about which you might actually want to receive e-mails from Facebook.

For RSS fans, you can also get notifications through an RSS feed that you subscribe to in Google Reader or another RSS reader. Go to your Notifications by clicking on the **Notifications icon** in the top blue navigation bar. At the bottom of the pop-up window that appears, you'll see **See all Notifications**. Click on that, and you'll see the full list of your notifications with a link labeled **RSS** near the top. It will take you to the RSS feed for your notifications and you can add it to your RSS reader. When you get a notification in Facebook, you will then see it automatically in your RSS reader without needing to go to Facebook to find it.

If you don't want to log into Facebook on a regular basis, the Notification options can give you a way to keep track of what is going on with your Friends through e-mail. If you already get too many e-mails, e-mail notifications probably will not be an attractive option, except for limited types of activities.

Mobile Apps

Many Facebook users—some estimates say more than half—use Facebook primarily on a mobile device. You can do this in one of two ways.

First, you can use your mobile device's browser to go to Facebook's website (**www.facebook.com**). If you do this, you will see a version of the Facebook site that is optimized for mobile devices. Second, and probably more popular, you can use the official Facebook mobile app to access your Facebook account. If you go to the App Store for your smart phone or tablet device (iPhone/iPad, Android, BlackBerry, and so on), you'll find an official Facebook app. It's free. You can download and install it. You'll set it up with your Facebook account information and password. We also discuss the mobile app and some alternatives in the Advanced Topics section on Facebook Apps in this book.

One you set it up, the App lets you access your Facebook account and see what is happening through a simple and easy-to-understand interface (see Figure 9.4). With the Facebook mobile app, you can get notifications on your mobile device and access your News Feed, invitations, Messages, and the like using your data plan—anytime, anywhere. Whenever you have a little downtime, are waiting in line or for an appointment, or are bored at an event, you can check your Facebook account, as you've undoubtedly seen many people doing these days. It's an easy, convenient, and mobile way to monitor what's happening in your Facebook network.

Benefits of Network Monitoring

As we like to emphasize, Facebook works best when it complements the real world. Great networkers are very aware of what is happening with the people in their networks and then acting on that information. Keeping up with Facebook happenings will let you know when to get in touch with Friends and give you something relevant to talk about

Figure 9.4: Official Facebook Mobile App for iPhone

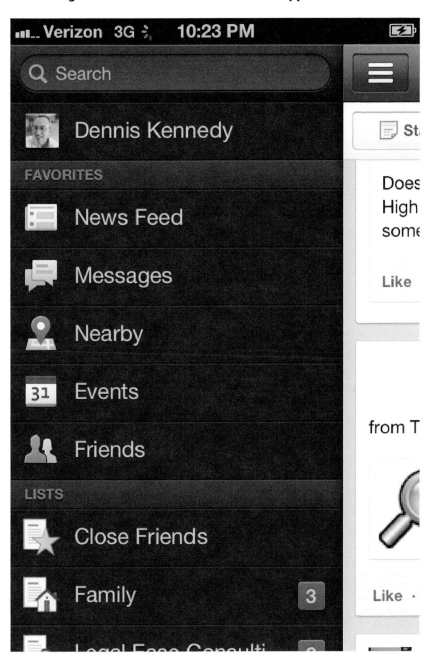

when you see them in the real world. For example, a Friend might post an Update about a job change. You might comment on the Update or send a message through Facebook. However, you can also do some traditional real-world networking by calling him or her, offering your congratulations, or extending an invitation to a celebratory lunch.

Monitoring your network should be a regular, ongoing process. Facebook does a lot of the work for you automatically with the tools we discussed in this Lesson. If you use them effectively, you can create value in and from your network.

Next, we introduce you to some additional features of the Facebook platform that illustrate the richness of the service and highlight some other features that might be especially useful for you.

Additional Features

You probably realize that Facebook is a rich platform with lots of features, many of which you had no idea existed before you read this book. In this section, we will briefly discuss some important things that didn't fit into our other Lessons or that we mentioned only briefly. We want you to be aware of them because one or more of them might be important to you, based on your circumstances and how you decide to use Facebook. The Facebook Help Center (**http://www.facebook.com/help/**) is the best place to get a better idea of what these features do, how they work, and the options you have when using them.

1. **Events.** Facebook has a robust and useful event/calendaring tool. You can use it to publicize and manage events that you create or use it in connection with events you have been invited to and plan to attend. To create an Event, click on Events or go to apps. You can create Events that are open or closed (for which the audience who can see, respond to, or attend is restricted), and you can use the Events app to manage guest lists and send messages to your guests. Your Events are visible from your Home Page.

2. **Photo and Video Publisher.** Although we refer to the photo and video publishing tools several places in the Lessons, we only touch on their capabilities. You can upload photos and videos, create photos and videos with your webcam for posting, create photo albums, edit information about the photos and videos, and more. For example, an immigration lawyer might create a short video about a new development in immigration law and get it quickly to

his or her Facebook audience to show expertise and start a conversation. Another tool to watch in this area is the new Facebook Camera tool. Facebook also bought a photo-sharing service called Instagram for one billion dollars, so it's clear that the importance of photos and videos in Facebook will continue to rise and we can expect to see even more improvements to these tools.

3. **Tagging.** Another interesting tool in Facebook is the ability to "tag" photos and videos. For example, if you have a class reunion photo or a photo taken at a reception held in your law office, you can, if appropriate, add tags to identify people in the photo. When a viewer rolls the mouse pointer over a tagged photo, the names of the tagged people appear in pop-up bubbles. Tagging can be used in several ways for many reasons. Since other people can tag you, there can be privacy concerns about tags, so be sure you understand the privacy settings for tags and adjust them to fit your preferences.

4. **Questions.** As a Group member or an individual, you can ask your audience a question and get their answers. Think of it as an informal survey tool. Questions can be a good tool to solicit feedback, gauge the interest of people in a topic, or generate conversation and discussions.

5. **Notes.** This app, found under APPS in the left column of your Home page, is intended for longer posts than the typical Update. Think of Notes as a mini-blog inside Facebook. If you want to make educational material about issues in your practice area available to your audience, Notes might be a great way to do that.

6. **Facebook Ads.** Facebook's internal ad system allows you to create ads and buy the right to place them in front of a focused target audience. Reportedly, these ads can be very successful for relatively minimal ad dollars. People have written whole books on Facebook ads, so there is a lot to learn, but Facebook ads might be a way to

announce a new business, promote an event, or otherwise market your practice—subject, of course, to the applicable ethics rules.

To learn more about Ads, go to **www.facebook.com/help/ads-and-business-solutions**. You'll need to create a title for your ad (twenty-five characters max) and some copy (135 characters max). Don't forget to include a call to action. Be concise but creative because ads are short and Facebook prohibits abbreviations and acronyms.

You can configure ads to pay by click or impression, beginning with $1 per day. Use pay-per-click if you're more concerned about getting traffic, or pay-per-impression if your main goal is visibility.

7. **Login to Other Accounts.** Don't you hate how many passwords you have to remember for all your different accounts? Wouldn't it be great if you had a single sign-on that worked for many different accounts? A surprising number of Internet services, especially social media platforms, will let you set up your account so you can use your Facebook credentials and password for your account with their service. It's an interesting approach, although you will want to consider carefully how the other services might use your Facebook login and whether they can post anything to your Facebook account. If it works for you, this feature can be a good way to reduce the number of usernames and passwords you have to remember.

8. **Children on Facebook.** There are huge issues involved with children being on Facebook. The terms of service prohibit children under age thirteen from creating accounts, and Facebook takes this limit very seriously. Unfortunately, there is a growing trend of parents allowing younger children to have a Facebook account and even facilitating the account set up. This is problematic on many levels. If you have young children who want you to help them set up a Facebook account, we recommend that you check with your

local police or sheriff's department (in the United States) to see if they give presentations to the public on these issues. In fact, we recommend such a presentation for any parent before letting children use the Internet.

Before allowing your teen to create a Facebook account, read a book like Pam Pearlman's *The Parent's Guide to Facebook: Tips and Strategies to Protect Your Children on the World's Largest Social Network*, make your child read it as a pre-requisite to getting the account, and then have "the talk" about Facebook safety. You need to establish rules and guidelines, set expectations, and determine consequences for breaking the rules.

Let's face it, you would not have wanted your parents to have access to your Facebook page when you were a teenager, so remember that many teens will be embarrassed to have parents as Friends. Worse yet, you might give them good reasons to be embarrassed. Many teens, however, will Friend relatives, so you will have some ways of checking on them. In any event, you will want to find a good way to balance your need to know what's going on with their needs for privacy and learning to be responsible.

9. **Facebook Interest Lists.** Similar to Twitter lists, interest lists are created by Facebook users to keep content on a particular subject or by a particular group of people in one place. When you subscribe to an interest list, you will receive some, but not all, posts from those lists on your Timeline. To see all of the posts from a particular list, click on the name of the Interest List on the left sidebar on your Home page. If you don't see it there or want more information, go to **www.facebook.com/help/search/?q=interest+lists**. You can also create your own interest lists.

Interest lists are good places to keep track of people who belong to a particular industry or post on a particular topic. They can be helpful for keeping client posts together or updates from people who provide information on practice management, marketing, potential blog topics, and so on. You can create lists of people in particular industries, which can make it easier to see what your target market is concerned about or struggling with.

10. **Facebook Places.** Facebook Places is a feature that allows you to "check in" on your mobile device to let people know where you are in real time. Once again, there are privacy and security issues that may arise here, so be careful when using this feature. It might be helpful to let people know where you are at a given time. Set privacy settings to **Places I check in to** and set it the way you want it—you may also want to look at the **Friends can check me into places** feature and disable it until you understand location services well enough to make an informed decisions about using them. Although you can always remove the tag, it's always better to be safe than sorry.

    You can also **claim your Place** for your law firm and link it to your Page if you would like Facebook users to be able to "check in" to your firm from their mobile device.

11. **Be Willing to Explore.** There is a lot going on in Facebook, definitely much more than this book can cover, and there's even more to come. We recommend that you explore and experiment in Facebook. Watch for announcements of new features. Become a student of Facebook. As we've mentioned, the Facebook Help Center is a great place to learn about Facebook features.

Finally, we wrap up the Lessons by drawing some conclusions about using Facebook and give you some important action steps you can take right away.

Developing a Strategic Approach and Three Easy Action Steps

Congratulations! You've learned the basics of the three aspects of Facebook that you must master: Identity (Profile/Timeline), Friends, and Participation. Now, it's time to put together a simple starting strategy for using Facebook and turn it into a great tool that works for you and your practice.

Purpose

Before you become active on Facebook, give some thought to your overall purpose and strategy: do you want to use Facebook mostly for connecting with friends and family, or are you seeking to use Facebook mostly to develop business, or something in between? That strategy will help you not only create your privacy and security settings, but also determine what to include in your Profile, who to invite to be your Friend, and how you participate.

Identity: Profile

The easiest place to begin is with your Profile. If you haven't already created your basic, bare-bones Facebook Profile, do that first. If you have a Profile already, now is the time to begin putting some meat on those bones and fleshing it out to give a more complete picture of who you are.

Make sure your profile includes:

- your Profile Picture (headshot) and an interesting Cover Photo
- information about your practice (even if you decide to use Facebook for purely personal reasons, you never know where business might come from)
- where you went to school
- information in the About section that helps give a well-rounded picture of who you are
- any necessary disclaimers

Identity Action Step: We suggest that you spend about an hour working on your Profile—in that time you can develop a profile that gives people who find you on Facebook a fairly good idea of who you are. Then you'll be ready to start inviting Friends.

Friends

If you wish, upload your contacts into Facebook. Otherwise, start with your real-world friends and colleagues and do some searches to see which ones are on Facebook. Then begin sending out Friend requests to those who have a Facebook account.

Search for potential connections by seeking out classmates, former colleagues, and members of groups you belong to (either online or off).

Add Friends gradually over time. We suggest that you begin by reviewing your contacts and sending five invitations weekly; also, using the **People You May Know** feature can be very helpful in finding Friends.

As your list of Friends grows, create Friend Lists to help target your posts and keep your Facebook activity germane to your different audiences.

Friends Action Step: Create a Friend List that helps you manage your Friends.

Participation

You will get the most out of Facebook if you actively participate and use it to create relationships. You have learned how to do that by joining and actively engaging with Groups, posting Updates (individual and firm-wide Page Updates), monitoring your News Feed, Commenting, Liking, and Sharing.

We recommend that at least weekly you post a brief Update and check your News Feed for interesting stories to Share or comment on Updates posted by your Friends. Using the **Like** button is a quick and easy way to stay engaged and connect with Friends without having to write something new yourself every time.

Take your Facebook relationships offline: send Friends e-mails, meet for coffee or lunch, or call them on the telephone. Make an effort to find out which of your Facebook Friends will be attending seminars or conferences you attend and plan to meet them in person. Send Updates asking people to contact you if they will be attending, see if the event has been posted on the Facebook Events application, and look for other attendees there. Or post the Event yourself and invite your Friends or only those on specific Friend Lists.

Participation Action Step: Try to develop a routine of posting three Updates each week and commenting on three of your Friends' Updates each week.

Building relationships takes time, whether in person or online. Use Facebook to identify and gain information about people you have just met or will be meeting. And keep using it to strengthen relationships and expand your network.

Participation in Facebook can help you identify and learn about potential clients, strategic alliances, and referral sources. Join Groups. They can be a good way to publicize what you are doing, build relationships, and establish your expertise. And, of course, Facebook can be a fun way to stay in touch with family and friends.

If you're looking for more than the basics on Facebook, move on to the Advanced Topics.

Ethics

In addition to being mindful of good social networking practices in general, lawyers also need to be keenly aware of the ethics rules that govern their activities. Some of those ethics rules will affect your Facebook participation. We encourage all lawyers to regularly review the ethics rules and recent ethics opinions in their jurisdictions, especially because many of those rules have not yet caught up with new technologies; some are being actively revised as this book is being written to include specific references to social media, including Facebook. Many state and local bar associations have issued ethics opinions specifically addressing Facebook, including New York City, Philadelphia, Florida, Texas, and Oregon, among others, and there are opinions in some jurisdictions about electronic communications and other social media outlets that may be instructive as well.

We'll cover some of the main ethics issues that may arise with lawyers' use of Facebook in this section, referring to the ABA Model Rules, but many states have different (and stricter) rules, so it is important that you become familiar with rules that apply to you. And, of course, we disclaim that we are giving any legal advice in this section. Rules and opinions do change, developments occur, and you will need to draw your own conclusions about the rules that apply to you and how to comply with them.

Ethics Summary

- Regulation of social media, including Facebook, is an evolving topic, so you must keep up to date on developments. Because of the increasing usage of Facebook by lawyers and a few highly publicized missteps some lawyers have already made, you are likely to see plenty of news coverage of any future developments that have a big impact on Facebook usage.
- Know and understand the opinions and approaches of the applicable jurisdictions for you and your practice.
- Follow the core principle of avoiding the dissemination of misleading information.
- Use appropriate and applicable disclaimers as required in your jurisdiction(s).
- Have a solid understanding of the advertising and solicitation rules, including those about specialties and endorsements.
- Implement a social media policy or add coverage of social media to existing firm policies.

False or Misleading Information

As a general rule, lawyers are prohibited from making false or misleading statements about themselves or their services. This rule is contained in ABA Model Rule 7.1.

In order to avoid being misleading, a lawyer or law firm must keep an online presence, including the Facebook Profile, Timeline, and Page, up to date and must ensure that disclaimers are included to prevent creating unjustified expectations in the mind of the website visitor (see Disclaimers in the next section).

If you post legal information on your Facebook Profile, Timeline, or Page, it might be wise to date the post and include a notice that the legal information was accurate as of the date of the writing, with a disclaimer that readers should not rely on the online information, but should instead consult a lawyer who can discuss their specific factual situation. This information may be added to your About section rather than made a part of each individual post. Outdated or inaccurate information should be removed wherever possible.

Disclaimers

ABA Model Rule 7.3(c) requires that every electronic communication from a lawyer soliciting professional employment from a prospective client known to be in need of legal services in a particular matter include the words *Advertising Material* unless it falls under one of the exceptions listed in Rule 7.3. Many jurisdictions share this requirement.

You can add a disclaimer to your About section. Add your required disclaimers, along with any instructions for those who want to contact you (you might refer them to your website or advise that you prefer rather than contact you through Facebook).

Whether your jurisdiction requires it or not, it is wise to include some kind of disclaimer on your Profile or Page indicating that visiting your Timeline, viewing presentations or other content, or contacting you through Facebook does not establish an attorney-client relationship, and that this contact may not be confidential. Make sure your disclaimers are clear and easy to understand.

Confidentiality

Confidentiality of client communications is one of the cornerstones of legal practice. ABA Model Rule 1.6 governs confidentiality of information and notes that a lawyer shall not reveal information relating to the representation of a client unless the client gives informed consent. Posting about client matters on your Timeline or within Groups—even without mentioning a client by name—can be problematic, especially if it's relatively easy to identify the client or matter from what you post.

Communications through Facebook can also raise confidentiality issues. Lawyers should take care to ensure that the confidentiality of communications with prospective clients is preserved. Lawyers should provide only general responses and should caution those asking questions on Facebook, whether within Groups, in Comments on a Timeline, or even in Messages, that confidentiality cannot be expected. If you do not fully understand privacy and other settings and how they work (discussed in Lesson 2), you should consider avoiding the use of Facebook for anything that might be confidential information. Also, be aware that some may argue that Facebook's privacy policy might also raise issues about the confidentiality of communications with clients through Facebook.

Friending current clients might also raise some confidentiality issues, particularly for clients with sensitive legal matters such as bankruptcy or divorce, although the risk might be somewhat diminished because the client must confirm any Friend request, thus indicating his or her willingness to be linked on Facebook.

In addition, it is unclear whether anyone looking at your Timeline or Friends would know that the individual was a client, as opposed to a neighbor, friend, colleague, co-worker, or so on. But consider confidentiality issues when requesting or accepting client Friend invitations. Check-ins or other indications of location might also raise confidentiality concerns.

Advertising

Most jurisdictions have special rules governing lawyer advertising. Are your Profile and Timeline considered advertising? In some jurisdictions they might be, depending on what content you post there. It would be difficult to argue that a law firm Page would not be advertising under the commonly understood definition. And, of course, Facebook ads must conform to the advertising rules.

The ABA issued an ethics opinion on lawyer websites, ABA Formal Opinion 10-457, in August of 2010, which provides that, if online activities promote a law practice, they are considered attorney advertising. That means that, if your Profile, Timeline, or Page promotes you as a lawyer, you should expect that it will be considered to be an advertisement and must comply with the advertising rules. Is a Facebook personal Profile simply informational or is it promotional? Reasonable minds can reach different conclusions. However, it's realistic to expect that bar regulators will err on the side of finding something to be advertising, based on what they've done in other Internet settings, especially given the general wariness they seem to have about Facebook.

ABA Model Rule 7.2 covers advertising. Rule 7.2(c) requires any communication considered advertising to include the name and office address of at least one lawyer or law firm responsible for its content. If your jurisdiction's rule is similar, and if your Profile, Timeline, or Updates can be considered advertising in your jurisdiction, be sure that your firm's office address appears somewhere in your Facebook Profile, and certainly include it on your Page.

Some states require prior review of advertisements or solicitations (for more on solicitations, see the next section), giving rise to questions about whether your Profile, Timeline, or Page would need to be reviewed before it could be posted or substantially updated, or whether embedded videos or presentations could be posted without prior review. For example, under Texas rule 7.07, law firm advertising must be submitted to the Advertising Review Committee. It has been determined that law firm or individual lawyer videos uploaded to Facebook must be submitted for review. It is unclear whether regular social networking Updates must also be submitted. Texas seems to have clarified that updates on certain social media sites, such as LinkedIn, do not, but you will, of course, need to confirm that for yourself and your jurisdiction.

Solicitation

Many states have special rules concerning solicitation, separate and apart from the general rules governing lawyer advertising. Generally, solicitation is distinguished from advertising because it involves direct contact with a specific person (or group of people) for the purpose of getting the lawyer hired, rather than an advertisement sent or available to the general public. Individual Friend requests or Messages through Facebook might be considered solicitations in some circumstances.

In 2010, the Philadelphia Bar Association issued an opinion (Philadelphia Bar Assn. Profl. Guidance Comm., Op. 2010-6) that its Rule 7.3 does not bar lawyers from using social media for solicitation where the prospective client has the ability to ignore the soliciting lawyer. Since those receiving Facebook Friend requests (or Messages) can ignore the request and simply not respond, this opinion might be read to permit lawyers to solicit using Facebook, subject, of course, to the applicable standard solicitation rules.

ABA Model Rule 7.3 governs direct contact with prospective clients. Subsection (a) prohibits "real time electronic contact to solicit professional employment from a prospective client when a significant motive for the lawyer's doing so is the lawyer's pecuniary gain" with specific exceptions. Subsection (c) requires any such communication to include a disclaimer (see the previous discussion on Disclaimers).

Specialization and "Expert" Status

Although lawyers are permitted to communicate the areas of law in which they practice, many jurisdictions prohibit lawyers from proclaiming that they are specialists or experts in any particular field, absent special certification by an approved, accredited authority. ABA Model Rule 7.4 also requires that the name of the accrediting organization be clearly identified. Lawyers should keep these rules in mind when completing their Profile and Page.

Inadvertent Attorney-Client Relationship and Unauthorized Practice of Law

Participating on social networking sites such as Facebook necessitates dissemination of your message to those outside of the jurisdiction where you practice. As such, you must be mindful of ABA Model Rule 5.5, which prohibits the unauthorized practice of law or practice outside of a jurisdiction in which you are admitted to practice.

You should also use caution when answering questions posed on Facebook, just as you would on sites such as Avvo or LinkedIn, to be sure that you are not creating an inadvertent attorney-client relationship or offering legal advice. ABA Formal Opinion 10-457 cites several cases from a variety of states noting that, because lawyers cannot screen for conflicts of interest when answering questions posted on the Internet, lawyers should refrain from answering specific legal questions unless the advice given is not fact-specific. However, it should be noted that many jurisdictions do permit lawyers to answer hypothetical questions.

In determining whether an attorney-client relationship has been established or a lawyer has violated the prohibition against unauthorized practice of law, the Rules and opinions place a great deal of importance upon who controls the flow of information and whether that information is provided unilaterally or whether it is part of a bilateral discussion, as well as the subsequent actions of the lawyer or firm once the communication is received (see ABA Formal Opinion 10-457 and ABA Model Rule 1.18). Remember that the existence of a client relationship is determined from the perspective of what the *client* thinks.

Likes and Recommendations

Some jurisdictions prohibit testimonials or recommendations entirely, while others allow them from former clients, but not current clients. Still others permit all testimonials. Most jurisdictions require some kind of disclaimer to accompany these testimonials.

It is unclear whether simply Liking a Page—or a post on a Timeline—would be considered a recommendation, testimonial, or endorsement, subject to the ethical rules governing recommendations and testimonials. As of this writing, we are unaware of any ethical opinion specifically addressing this topic.

These issues may be particularly troublesome for Pages because Pages are public—posts on them can be seen by everyone. Lawyers are responsible not only for what they publish on the web about themselves, but also for what others publish about them. A glowing endorsement from a client on your Page could create an ethical issue. As noted in Lesson 4, we recommend that lawyers set their Pages to hide posts by others until they can be reviewed by the Page Administrator to ensure compliance. For example, during a review, a lawyer should add a disclaimer where appropriate and check that clients do not use words that ethical rules prohibit lawyers themselves from using. Some firms may choose to disable the ability of others to post to their Page entirely.

The general standard is that, so long as the statement can be objectively proven, it is permissible. Phrases like "best tax lawyer in America" or "most awesome real estate lawyer ever" would not meet the objectively provable standard. You must also be sure that the post cannot be considered false or misleading.

Lawyers should also be aware of the ethical rules when placing Like and Recommend buttons on their other sites. Like and Recommend buttons allow people to share content they find in other places on the web with their Facebook Friends. Clicking on **Like** or **Recommend** buttons will create a story on the individual's Timeline and may appear in News Feeds in the same way that Likes do.

According to ABA Model Rule 7.2(b), lawyers are prohibited from giving anything of value to a person for recommending the lawyer's services. How does that impact your Facebook participation? Don't offer reciprocal Likes or endorsements on Facebook Pages ("you recommend me and I'll recommend you").

Using Facebook as an Investigation Tool

We discuss Facebook in litigation and discovery in another Advanced Topics chapter in this book. Facebook can be a useful tool for gathering information in litigation, but you must be aware of the ethical boundaries of doing so.

For example, ABA Model Rule 4.2 forbids communication with a person represented by another lawyer, which may limit the ability of a lawyer (or someone acting on the lawyer's behalf, including an outside investigator) to access a party's posts on Facebook. If a post is Public, it may be fair game (see Oregon State Bar Association Opinion No. 2005-164, August 2005). But a lawyer attempting to Friend a represented party would be in violation of the ethical prohibition in Rule 4.2 (see, for example, Oregon State Bar Opinion No. 2005-164, August 2005 and San Diego County Bar Association Ethics Opinion 2011-2, May 2011).

Similarly, attempting to obtain information on Facebook from an unrepresented party or witness may implicate Model Rule 4.1(a), which precludes a lawyer from making "a false statement of material fact or law to a third person," and Rule 8.4(c) (noted above). Opinions from the Philadelphia Bar Association and the New York City Bar differ on what is permitted in this context.

Friending potential jurors is also considered improper contact and an ethical violation. Friending judges, opposing counsel, and experts might give rise to ethical issues as well. For example, consider Rule 3.5 on Impartiality and Decorum of the Tribunal, which prohibits lawyers from seeking to influence or communicate ex parte with judges and jurors.

General Tips

The best rule of thumb when considering what you can and cannot do on Facebook (or any other social networking site) is not to say anything that you wouldn't be comfortable saying or doing in a room full of people or publishing on the front page of *The New York Times*.

Make sure you have a social media policy for your law firm that clearly spells out the firm's guidelines for use of social media by everyone in the office. Watch out for specialized issues that arise out of social media usage. For example, the use of social media by and with judges has already raised a number of questions.

Become familiar with the ethical rules in your jurisdiction about Friending (especially with respect to clients or judges) and using social media as an investigative tool in connection with potential jurors, witnesses, and opposing parties.

Final Thought

In many ways, behavior in Facebook and social media is identical, at least conceptually, to behavior in the physical world, and the same ethical principles apply. When considering Facebook activities, think about the ethical implications of comparable real-world activities. If you take that approach, stay mindful of the basic principle of avoiding misrepresentation, and stay aware of your state's specific rules or guidelines, you should be in good shape on the ethical front.

However, social media is constantly evolving, and we expect that ethics regulations will continue to evolve as regulators understand social media tools better than they do now. As in the real world, you must keep up to date on current developments, such as the ABA's ongoing Ethics 20/20 effort (**http://www.americanbar.org/groups/professional_ responsibility/aba_commission_on_ethics_20_20.html**).

Separating Your Personal from Your Professional Presence

One of the main concerns we hear from lawyers about using Facebook (aside from the privacy and security concerns) is how to keep their personal and professional lives separate. We'll try to address these concerns and provide some options for how to do that. But first, we encourage lawyers to consider whether they actually *want* to separate the personal from the professional on Facebook and, if so, how much.

In the real world, are your personal and professional lives entirely separate, or do they overlap? Do you receive referrals from friends, relatives, and neighbors? When you converse with clients and professional colleagues, is it strictly business all of the time, or do you relate to them on a more human and personal level? Do you ever discuss vacations, children, or hobbies with professional contacts? For most lawyers, there is at least *some* overlap between the personal and the professional. There is no compelling reason that your online activities, including your use of Facebook, can't mix the personal and the professional as well.

Business Pages vs. Personal Profiles

One way to create some separation between the personal and the professional, particularly for solo and small-firm lawyers, is to create both a personal Profile and a law firm Page.

Use your Page to post firm news and share links to firm publications. Create Events on Facebook to coincide with live events in which the Firm participates. Publicize those Events on the firm's Page. Use the firm's Page to interact with industry insiders, referral sources, strategic alliances, and even clients. The firm can strictly control who may post on the firm's Page and act as a Page Administrator, moderating the content of posts to keep them strictly firm-related and professional. For more ideas about what to do with the firm's Page, see Lesson 4.

By contrast, the individual lawyers' Profiles and Timelines can be less formal and contain more personal information and personal posts. Lawyers would then use the personal Profile rather than the firm's Page to interact with real-life friends on a more personal level, post vacation or family pictures, and talk about hobbies and interests. To connect to the firm, individual lawyers would simply Like the firm's Page and list the firm in the employment section of their Profiles, which would link the individual to the firm's Page.

Potential Drawbacks

One of the major drawbacks of attempting to separate your personal and professional use of Facebook by using your Profile for strictly personal reasons and your Page for strictly professional reasons is that, although Pages can Like other Pages and receive their Updates in the Page's News Feed, a Page cannot Friend a personal Profile and, thus, cannot receive Updates from individuals. To receive Updates from clients, colleagues, and industry insiders in your News Feed, you need to do it as an individual.

In addition, Pages cannot communicate individually with those who Like the Page unless the individual sends the Page a private Message, in which case the Page can send a private Message in return.

Using Facebook Friend Lists

Another way to separate the personal from the professional on Facebook, particularly for lawyers in larger firms who may not have control over or the ability to post to their firm's Page, is to make use of Friend Lists, as we discussed in Lesson 6.

Restricting the Post Audience

Friend Lists help you segregate your messages and control who sees which posts on your Timeline. For example, you might post a personal Update on Facebook that you want only family and close friends to see, but you don't want to share it with clients, referral sources, or colleagues from your firm. In that case, you would make the Update visible only to your list of close family and friends, or hide the post from lists containing clients, and so on.

You can also restrict your Updates that relate to work and that only your professional colleagues would be interested in so you don't turn off friends and family with technical legal information. As we discussed in Lesson 7, your post privacy will remain in place, even for Comments and Likes.

You can create a different Friend List for strategic alliances and other professionals, a second specifically for other lawyers in your area of practice, one for law school classmates, and so on. People can be added to more than one Friend List. Remember, however, that Friends can share your posts outside of the Friend List.

Reviewing Posts from Friend Lists

Friend Lists can also help you filter what you read on Facebook. After you have created lists, you can see them in the left column on your Home page in the News Feed. Clicking on a particular list brings you to a page that contains only Updates from that list. This makes finding posts from a particular group much easier than scrolling through your entire News Feed.

When you are in work mode or want to interact on Facebook with professional colleagues to see what they are up to, view the Friend Lists containing your work colleagues and respond to them or send Updates only to that list; when you're in "play" mode, you can look at Friend lists of your college buddies or your Saturday night bowling league and interact with them. But, as with all networking, keep in mind that business can come from anywhere, and you should always be a professional, even in a more relaxed setting. Using good judgment is essential, no matter what approach you take to separating the personal and professional.

Facebook Apps

Facebook offers millions of Apps. Some of them can enhance your experience. Some can create unexpected problems. Some might be considered productivity apps. Many are games. As we mentioned in Lesson 2 on settings, you must learn exactly what permissions you are giving Apps, what data they can access, and what they can send out on your behalf. Do you really want all your Friends to know that you had a successful night playing poker, bought some cows in Farmville, watched an inappropriate video, or got a new high score in a game?

We divide Facebook Apps into two categories: first, the official Facebook mobile App for smartphones (discussed in Lesson 9) and third-party alternatives to the official mobile App and, second, Apps that run inside Facebook (we'll refer to them as Facebook Apps).

We enthusiastically recommend that you install and use the official Facebook mobile app or an alternative for reasons we discussed in Lesson 9. We also recommend that you consider trying a few Facebook Apps—carefully.

Mobile Apps

There is an official Facebook App for all of the smartphone and tablet platforms (iOS, Android, BlackBerry, and so on). It's free and can be downloaded and installed from the applicable App Store. Once installed, you can access and use your Facebook account on your mobile device. You might even find this experience better than using the Facebook website with the browser on your computer.

The official Facebook Mobile App is quite good, laid out logically, and easy to use. We use it regularly and are happy with it. Some people do have complaints about certain aspects of the official Facebook mobile app, so be aware that there are alternatives like Friendly for Facebook (**www.oecoway.com/**), Friendcaster (**friendcasterapp.com/**), and Seesmic (**seesmic.com/seesmic-social/mobile/**).

Facebook has also launched a brand new Pages Manager app. As of this writing, it is only available for iPhone, but it wouldn't surprise us if other versions are released soon. Pages Manager helps Page Administrators respond to comments, post to the Page, and receive Page notifications, among other features. Pages Manager is free.

Facebook Apps

Facebook Apps are small programs than run in your Facebook environment and often are designed to improve your Facebook experience or pull in data from other sources to display on your Timeline, Updates, or elsewhere. There are also many games, the most famous of which include Farmville and Words with Friends.

By way of illustration, Dennis has used the Twitter Facebook App almost as long as he has been on Facebook. This app connects his personal Twitter account to Facebook. His tweets on Twitter automatically show up on Facebook as Updates, eliminating the need to type the posts in two separate places or copy and paste them. There are advantages and disadvantages to this approach because his Twitter and Facebook audiences are different, but the App is an example of an easy way to use a Facebook App to pull other aspects of your social media or Internet presence into Facebook.

Probably the best way to learn about Facebook Apps before jumping in and getting started is to take a quick walk through the Facebook Help Center to learn about Apps and Games. Click on the **inverted triangle** at the right side of the top blue navigation bar. The last option is "Help." Click on it and you'll be taken to the Facebook Help Center (see Figure Apps-1).

Figure Apps-1: Facebook Help Center

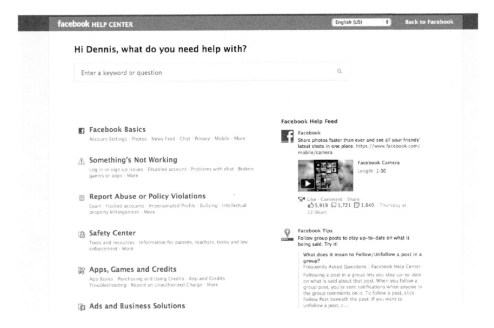

Click on **Apps, Games, and Credits** and you'll see all kinds of useful information about Apps and Games (see Figure Apps-2). Spend some time here before you start installing any app or game.

Trying to locate a Facebook App can be a little daunting because of the sheer volume of Apps. There are currently millions of Apps, including those for individual accounts and for Pages.

Figure Apps-2: Apps, Games, and Credits

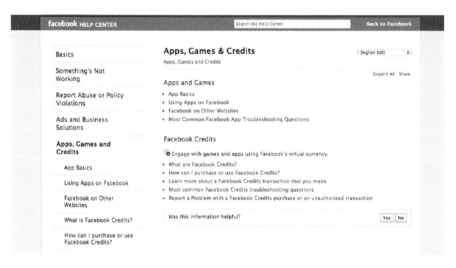

Start out by going to your Home page (click on **Home** in the top blue navigation bar). In the left column, look for **APPS**. Click on **Apps and Games** under it (see Figure Apps-3).

Figure Apps-3: Apps and Games Page

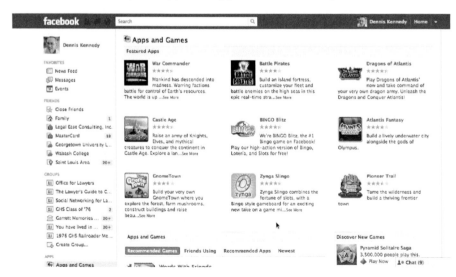

Here you see two categories of Facebook Apps. First, there is a section of Featured Apps. Think of these as the Apps that Facebook thinks are hot. You might or might not have any interest in these, but it can be a way to find a popular new app quickly.

The second section is called Apps and Games. It has four links under it: Recommended Games, Friends Using, Recommended Apps, and New. You can look through these categories to find Facebook Apps that might interest you. The Friends Using category can be helpful if you have friends who are savvy Facebook users.

Before installing any Facebook App, we recommend that you do your homework and look for reviews, known problems, and any discussion of privacy or other issues. We cannot overemphasize how important it is to understand how apps work, how they access and use your data, and how to set your privacy settings.

When you install a Facebook App, you will have choices to make for five key settings on permissions:

- Can the App access your basic Facebook information—the directory information that Facebook requires to be public?
- Can the App send you e-mail?
- Can the App post to Facebook as you?
- Can the App access your information on Facebook anytime, including when you aren't logged into Facebook?
- Can the App publish your activity using the game or App?

Some apps might also ask to access your Timeline information or information people share with you. Consider carefully the consequences of each permission setting and do not accept defaults without reading them.

Using Facebook Apps can be an easy and free way to enhance your Facebook experience and effectiveness. We recommend that you carefully consider trying a few of them.

Litigation and Discovery

The role of social media data, such as that on Facebook, has recently become a very hot topic in the worlds of litigation and e-discovery. If you are a litigator or a lawyer who must advise a client about litigation or records management, it is essential to have an understanding of how Facebook works, even if you don't use Facebook yourself. However, if you actually use Facebook, you'll understand it in practical ways that will undoubtedly help you and your clients in the litigation context.

The idea of using Facebook data in litigation matters is attractive to lawyers and easy to illustrate. Imagine someone claiming a permanent, disabling injury preventing him or her from doing any work who posts pictures showing just the opposite or who posts an update that reads, "OMG! I ran into someone's car today and it was my fault."

Many Facebook users do not properly use privacy and account settings, so Facebook has become an attractive place to look for relevant information in litigation matters. It's difficult to imagine a litigation matter in which it wouldn't make sense to take a little time to check Facebook for information about the people involved in the case. However, be mindful of potential ethical issues.

If you've read Lesson 2 and considered some of the other points we've made about Facebook privacy, you will realize that, in many cases, the discovery of this type of Facebook information is largely attributable to the use of Public or other overly broad settings. With well-chosen privacy settings, outsiders who are not Friends should not have access to a user's content.

Facebook might also be useful for learning relevant information about the connections people have, other information about experts and other witnesses, and the like. It's also clear that some lawyers are checking Facebook in connection with jury selection. We recommend that you read the discussion of ethics in this book before launching into these kinds of activities.

Not surprisingly, Facebook has developed procedures for dealing with requests for information. The easiest way to find their current policies is to go to the Facebook Help Center and do a search on "subpoena" (see Figure Lit-1).

Figure Lit-1: "Subpoena" Search Results

At the time of this writing, Facebook says to allow thirty days for them to respond to a subpoena. Note that Facebook treats basic account information differently from actual content (Messages, Time-line posts, Photos, and so on). Facebook will provide some account information if you can sufficiently identify the account holder by providing the e-mail address, Facebook user ID (UID), and vanity URL, if any. (Names, birthdays, locations, and other information are insufficient to identify a Facebook account). The requested information must be "indispensable" to the case, and you must personally serve Facebook with a California or federal subpoena.

On the other hand, Facebook says that federal law (e.g., the Stored Communications Act, 18 U.S.C. § 2701 *et seq.*) prohibits it from disclosing account content (Messages, Updates, Photos, and so on) to a nongovernmental entity pursuant to a civil subpoena or court order. Facebook notes that the account user has a "download user data" option to obtain and provide content in the course of a litigation matter. By understanding this, a lawyer can determine the best way to obtain content from the account owner.

We are clearly at the opening stages of the use of Facebook and other social media information in litigation and discovery. There are many questions that are only beginning to be answered, such as:

- Can you be forced to turn over your account password?
- What Facebook data might be considered a "record" for records management purposes?
- What contacts (including Friending), if any, can lawyers have through Facebook during the course of litigation?

By understanding how Facebook works, especially by using it yourself, you'll be able to understand the questions that arise, determine the value of Facebook data in matters, and protect your clients who use Facebook. As with any new technology, our best advice is to keep a close eye out for any developments in the area of Facebook and litigation.

Tips

1) Check Facebook's Help materials (**http://www.facebook.com/help/**).

2) Because Facebook has been around for a long time, many other people may have had the same question you have. Check Facebook's Community Forum (**http://www.facebook.com/help/ community/**) and the Help Feed on the Help page to find answers to frequently asked questions (**http://www.facebook.com/help**) to see if you can find the answer to your question.

3) Turn on the Secure Browsing option if there is any chance whatsoever that you will access your Facebook account over Public WiFi.

4) Take the time to walk through all of your privacy and account settings and consider each choice. Then revisit these settings on a regular basis and any time you learn that Facebook has made a change to its approach to privacy.

5) Use a *strong* password (combinations of upper and lower case letter, numbers, and symbols) on your account and change it on a regular basis.

6) Think carefully about whether you want to keep your professional life and personal life separate. Lawyers tend to use LinkedIn as a professional presence and Facebook for a personal presence. But if you want to use Facebook both personally and professionally, you can do so by creating lists, targeting the messages you send out to different audiences, and creating a Page for your law firm.

7) Take time to consider what approach you want to take to Friending people, especially clients and co-workers. Have a plan for

adding Friends (i.e., quality or quantity, local or global, inside your current organization or outside).

8) Especially for lawyers, understanding and using Friend Lists to control what certain groups of Friends see and receive is very important.

9) Become familiar with your jurisdiction's ethics rules affecting Facebook participation and monitor developments.

10) Take your Facebook relationships offline—use Facebook to identify people with whom you can have lunch or attend a seminar or event.

11) When traveling, search your Friends to see which of your Friends live where you will be visiting and try to get together while you're in town.

12) Schedule regular weekly or monthly time for Facebook activities, including visiting your News Feed, Liking or Commenting on others' Status Updates, and posting your own Updates, Photos, and links.

13) Consider your audience with everything you post to Facebook. Develop a good understanding of who can see each type of activity in which you engage on Facebook. Assume that everything you post will be seen by the people you'd least like to see it. Good judgment is paramount.

14) Use the excellent Facebook feature that lets you see exactly how other people see your Facebook Timeline and other Facebook information. From the **Timeline**, find the **gear icon** and click **View as**.

15) Create a separate Page for your law firm, but be careful who you designate as Page Administrator(s). Set appropriate permissions levels.

16) Take advantage of Facebook's new administrator roles to give different levels of permissions to lawyers and staff in your firm so they can help manage your Page.

17) Use search features to find people to Friend or Subscribe.

18) Use Updates to send news and relevant links of value to your network.

19) Post self-promotion, business-related, and business-seeking Updates sparingly, self-deprecatingly, and subtly on Facebook. Most Facebook users expect to see personal updates. Always think about the actual value to others you bring and think about how you would react to someone else doing the same thing.

20) Add any necessary legal disclaimers to your Profile and Page. Use the About section of your firm's Page for disclaimers and other material required under applicable ethics rules.

21) Think about syncing your blog, LinkedIn, and Twitter accounts to Facebook to allow for cross-posting and to get a bigger audience for information you post in other places. But be aware of how you use each service to assure that all posts will be appropriate for all audiences.

22) Subscribe to the public Updates of individuals who interest you, but who you do not think would Friend you (or who you don't want to Friend). This is a great way to see what experts in your field are saying even though you are not Friends.

23) Enable the Subscriptions and Messages settings to allow others to receive your public Updates and send you private Messages through Facebook.

24) Put links to your Facebook account and Like buttons on your website, blog, social media profiles, e-mail signature, or other places you can be found on the Internet to let people get to you and interact with you on Facebook no matter how they find you on the Internet.

25) The official Facebook mobile app is excellent and free. Download and install it.

26) Although you can start with a good personal photograph, invest in some good professional photographs to use on Facebook. Make sure your face is large enough to be recognizable.

27) It is OK to use personal photos, vacation photos, and photos with other people in them on Facebook, but think about the message they convey.

28) Decide what you want to do about connecting with colleagues at your present employer (the "Do I friend my boss?" issue). Your approach can make a big difference when you want to look for a new job and can affect what you feel comfortable posting.

29) Always keep the real-world analogies in mind when using Facebook. If you are circumspect in connecting with, or giving personal information to, people in the real world, you will probably be most comfortable taking a similar approach on Facebook.

30) If you are speaking at a conference or other event, use the Events feature to help promote the event or invite others to attend.

31) Get a Facebook badge for your website that will direct visitors to your Facebook Page. You can get it by visiting **http://www.facebook.com/badges/page.php**.

32) Do not underestimate the value of Facebook in helping help you reconnect with people who were important in your life, including in your legal career, but with whom you have lost contact.

33) To remove someone from your People You May Know list (either those you know you will not want to send a Friend request, or those you are sure you do not know), roll your mouse over the box containing their information and click the ✕.

34) Use the Find Friends from Different Parts of Your Life tool to grow Friend Lists and Groups quickly and easily.

35) Add backdated Events and Photos to the Timeline for your firm's Page to create a rich sense of history and accomplishment for your firm.

36) Tread cautiously if you want to use location tools and either check-in to places yourself or let others check you into places. Your location might reveal much more than you expect.

37) Join Groups to gather and sustain relevant groups of people in your network. If you're not sure where to start with Groups, join our Social Networking for Lawyers Group.

38) Share content generated by your Friends and those to whom you Subscribe by using the Share button. This has the double benefit of providing value to your network, and it is a good way to compliment and get the attention of people you respect and want to know better.

39) Use the drop-down context menu to the right of each post in your News Feed to control what kind of Updates you receive from an individual Friend.

40) Take advantage of the context menu when you receive updates from Friends about games or apps. Get rid of them by clicking on **hide all Updates from** that game or app.

41) Use Friend Lists not only to control what content you send out, but what content you see. Segregate your News Feed to see only posts from people on a particular Friend List by clicking on the name of that List in the left navigation bar of your Home page.

42) If you are an Administrator of your law firm Page or a Page for another organization, download the Facebook Pages Manager app to manage or post as your Page on the go.

43) Change the order of the tabs or Apps that appear on your Page's Timeline by hovering your mouse pointer over them and clicking on the **pencil icon** to edit.

44) Create calls to action or direct visitors to specific landing pages on Facebook or on your website by customizing your App tabs on your Timeline. Click the **pencil icon** and go to **Edit Settings**.

45) Remember that the person who originally creates a post or Update controls its visibility, and they can change the visibility by returning to the post later and editing it. Always assume when you comment on another's post that it can be seen publicly, regardless of the initial visibility setting.

46) Review Facebook's rules about Pages, particularly the prohibitions relating to Cover Photos.

47) Before calling, e-mailing, or meeting in person with a Friend, check the Friend's Timeline to get an idea of what they are doing and to find good topics of conversation.

48) Consider using a Group to create a "living," interactive version of your standard firm or practice group newsletter.

49) When you receive a Friend invitation, look at the list of mutual Friends to: (a) determine whether people you trust have already Friended the person; and (b) get some ideas for other people you should invite to be Friends.

50) Read your News Feed and the Updates in them to get an idea of the tone and topics your Friends use before diving in with a lot of Updates of your own.

51) If you are a litigator, become familiar with Facebook's subpoena policy.

52) Give some thought to whether you want to post to Facebook during normal business hours and the perception that might be created if you do so.

53) If you have a social media policy, take care to follow it. Set the tone by your example.

54) Realize that, for some people, especially younger people, Messages, not e-mail, might be the preferred manner of communication and the fastest (or only) way to get a reply.

55) Post something in the past that you regret? You can go back and hide or limit the audience for past posts.

56) Apps can be useful, but make sure you understand exactly what they do and what you are giving them permission to do on your behalf.

57) If you have a Page, use other communications, especially non-Internet communications (business cards, letterhead, and so on) to let people know about the Page and link to the Page from your existing website.

58) You can use the Go Online setting to chat in real time, including video chat, with other Friends who are online.

59) Learning the basic navigation scheme of Facebook can be a big help. There are often several ways to accomplish the same task.

60) Moving your mouse pointer in Facebook and hovering over spaces (usually to the right of a link) often will bring up a context-related menu of options much like right-clicking a mouse will do in most standard computer programs.

Resources

Official Facebook Resources

Facebook Blog, http://blog.facebook.com/

Facebook Help Center, http://www.facebook.com/help/

To learn more about the new format for Facebook Pages, visit these resources:

- www.facebook.com/about/page
- www.facebook.com/help/pages/new-design
- www.facebook.com/page_guidelines.php

External Resources

ABA Ethics 20/20 Commission, http://www.americanbar.org/groups/professional_responsibility/aba_commission_on_ethics_20_20.html.

ABA Ethics 20/20 Commission Initial Draft Proposals on Lawyers' Use of Technology and Client Development, June 29, 2011, http://www.americanbar.org/content/dam/aba/administrative/ethics_2020/20110629ethics202technologyclientdevelopment initialresolutionsandreport.authcheckdam.pdf.

ABA Formal Opinion 10-457, Lawyer Websites, issued in August 2010, http://www.americanbar.org/content/dam/aba/migrated/cpr/pdfs/10_457.authcheckdam.pdf.

ABA Journal, Seduced: For Lawyers, the Appeal of Social Media Is Obvious. It's Also Dangerous, February 2011, http://www.aba journal.com/magazine/article/seduced_for_lawyers_the_appeal_of_social_media_is_obvious_dangerous/.

ABA Model Rules of Professional Conduct, http://www.americanbar. org/groups/professional_responsibility/publications/model_rules_ of_professional_conduct/model_rules_of_professional_conduct_ table_of_contents.html.

Carolyn Abram, *Facebook for Dummies* (For Dummies, 2012).

Albert-Laszlo Barabasi, *Linked: How Everything Is Connected to Everything Else and What It Means* (Plume, 2003).

Debra Bruce, 12 Social Media Ethics Issues for Lawyers, *SoloPractice- University*, http://solopracticeuniversity.com/2010/03/11/a-dozen- social-media-ethics-issues-for-lawyers/.

Garrick Chow, Facebook Essential Training Video, *Lynda.com*, http://www.lynda.com/Facebook-training/Essential-Training/ 80434-2C.html.

Electronic Frontier Foundation, Social Media, https://www.eff.org/ issues/social-networks.

Carolyn Elefant and Nicole Black, *Social Media for Lawyers: The Next Frontier* (American Bar Association, 2010).

Michelle Golden, *Social Media Strategies for Professionals and Their Firms: The Guide to Establishing Credibility and Accelerating Rela- tionships* (Wiley Professional Advisory, 2010).

Law Practice magazine, The Social Media Issue, January/February 2012, http://www.americanbar.org/publications/law_practice_ magazine/2012/january_february.html.

Lindsey Griffiths, Facebook Tutorials, *Zen & the Art of Legal Market- ing Blog*, http://www.zenlegalnetworking.com/tags/facebook- tutorials/.

Bryn Hughes, Think social media is a waste of time? Your competitors don't . . . *The Official Blog of Martindale-Hubbell*, http://blog. martindale.com/think-social-media-is-a-waste-of-time-your- competitors-dont.

Inside Facebook, http://www.insidefacebook.com/.

The Kennedy-Mighell Report Podcast, "Who Moved My Social Media Cheese?" http://legaltalknetwork.com/podcasts/kennedy-mighell-report/2011/12/who-moved-my-social-media-cheese/.

David Kirkpatrick, *The Facebook Effect: The Inside Story of the Company That Is Connecting the World* (Simon & Schuster, 2011).

Evan Koblentz, Lexis Says Social Networking Lags at Large Firms, *Law Technology News* (December 13, 2011), http://www.law.com/jsp/lawtechnologynews/PubArticleLTN.jsp?id=1202535285157.

Harvey Mackay, *Dig Your Well Before You're Thirsty: The Only Networking Book You'll Ever Need* (Currency Books, 1999).

Joshua Poje, Legal Ethics and Policy Considerations in E-Communications and Social Media, *ABA Legal Technology Resource Center*, http://www.iml.org/files/pages/4213/LegalEthicsSocialMedia.pdf.

Allison C. Shields and Dennis Kennedy, Facebook for Lawyers, (Audio), http://www.ali-aba.org/index.cfm?fuseaction=courses.course&course_code=RSTP18.

Clara Shih, *The Facebook Era: Tapping Online Social Networks to Market, Sell, and Innovate* (Addison-Wesley Professional, 2010).

Marty Weintraub, *Killer Facebook Ads: Master Cutting-Edge Facebook Advertising Techniques* (Sybex, 2011).

Nicholas, "Top 10 Most Requested Facebook Tips," http://www.online-tech-tips.com/computer-tips/10-most-requested-facebook-tips/.

Index

SELECTED BOOKS FROM

iPad in One Hour for Lawyers, Second Edition
By Tom Mighell
Product Code: 5110747 / LPM Price: $24.95 / Regular Price: $39.95

Whether you are a new or a more advanced iPad user, *iPad in One Hour for Lawyers* takes a great deal of the mystery and confusion out of using your iPad. Ideal for lawyers who want to get up to speed swiftly, this book presents the essentials so you don't get bogged down in technical jargon and extraneous features and apps. In just six, short lessons, you'll learn how to:

- Quickly Navigate and Use the iPad User Interface
- Set Up Mail, Calendar, and Contacts
- Create and Use Folders to Multitask and Manage Apps
- Add Files to Your iPad, and Sync Them
- View and Manage Pleadings, Case Law, Contracts, and other Legal Documents
- Use Your iPad to Take Notes and Create Documents
- Use Legal-Specific Apps at Trial or in Doing Research

Google for Lawyers: Essential Search Tips and Productivity Tools
By Carole A. Levitt and Mark E. Rosch
Product Code: 5110704 / LPM Price: $47.95 / Regular Price: $79.95

This book introduces novice Internet searchers to the diverse collection of information locatable through Google. The book discusses the importance of including effective Google searching as part of a lawyer's due diligence, and cites case law that mandates that lawyers should use Google and other resources available on the Internet, where applicable. For intermediate and advanced users, the book unlocks the power of various advanced search strategies and hidden search features they might not be aware of.

iPad Apps in One Hour for Lawyers
By Tom Mighell
Product Code: 5110739 / LPM Price: $19.95 / Regular Price: $34.95

At last count, there were more than 80,000 apps available for the iPad. Finding the best apps often can be an overwhelming, confusing, and frustrating process. iPad Apps in One Hour for Lawyers provides the "best of the best" apps that are essential for any law practice. In just one hour, you will learn about the apps most worthy of your time and attention. This book will describe how to buy, install, and update iPad apps, and help you:

- Find apps to get organized and improve your productivity
- Create, manage, and store documents on your iPad
- Choose the best apps for your law office, including litigation and billing apps
- Find the best news, reading, and reference apps
- Take your iPad on the road with apps for travelers
- Maximize your social networking power
- Have some fun with game and entertainment apps during your relaxation time

The Electronic Evidence and Discovery Handbook: Forms, Checklists, and Guidelines
By Sharon D. Nelson, Bruce A. Olson, and John W. Simek
Product Code: 5110569 / LPM Price: $99.95 / Regular Price: $129.95

The use of electronic evidence has increased dramatically over the past few years, but many lawyers still struggle with the complexities of electronic discovery. This substantial book provides lawyers with the templates they need to frame their discovery requests and provides helpful advice on what they can subpoena. In addition to the ready-made forms, the authors also supply explanations to bring you up to speed on the electronic discovery field. The accompanying CD-ROM features over 70 forms, including, Motions for Protective Orders, Preservation and Spoliation Documents, Motions to Compel, Electronic Evidence Protocol Agreements, Requests for Production, Internet Services Agreements, and more. Also included is a full electronic evidence case digest with over 300 cases detailed!

The Lawyer's Guide to Microsoft Word 2010
By Ben M. Schorr
Product Code: 5110721 / LPM Price: $41.95 / Regular Price: $69.95

Microsoft® Word is one of the most used applications in the Microsoft® Office suite. This handy reference includes clear explanations, legal-specific descriptions, and time-saving tips for getting the most out of Microsoft Word®—and customizing it for the needs of today's legal professional. Focusing on the tools and features that are essential for lawyers in their everyday practice, this book explains in detail the key components to help make you more effective, more efficient, and more successful.

LinkedIn in One Hour for Lawyers
By Dennis Kennedy and Allison C. Shields
Product Code: 5110737 / LPM Price: $19.95 / Regular Price: $34.95

Lawyers work in a world of networks, connections, referrals, and recommendations. For many lawyers, the success of these networks determines the success of their practice. LinkedIn®, the premier social networking tool for business, can help you create, nurture, and expand your professional network and gain clients in the process. LinkedIn® in One Hour for Lawyers provides an introduction to this powerful tool in terms that any attorney can understand. In just one hour, you will learn to:

- Set up a LinkedIn account
- Complete your basic profile
- Create a robust, dynamic profile that will attract clients
- Build your connections
- Use search tools to enhance your network
- Maximize your presence with features such as groups, updates, answers, and recommendations
- Monitor your network with ease
- Optimize your settings for privacy concerns
- Use LinkedIn® effectively in the hiring process
- Develop a LinkedIn strategy to grow your legal network

SELECTED BOOKS FROM

LawPracticeManagementSection
MARKETING • MANAGEMENT • TECHNOLOGY • FINANCE

Virtual Law Practice:
How to Deliver Legal Services Online
By Stephanie L. Kimbro

Product Code: 5110707 / LPM Price: $47.95 / Regular Price: $79.95

The legal market has recently experienced a dramatic shift as lawyers seek out alternative methods of practicing law and providing more affordable legal services. Virtual law practice is revolutionizing the way the public receives legal services and how legal professionals work with clients. If you are interested in this form of practicing law, *Virtual Law Practice* will help you:

- *Responsibly deliver legal services online to* your clients
- Successfully set up and operate a virtual law office
- Establish a virtual law practice online through a secure, client-specific portal
- Manage and market your virtual law practice
- Understand state ethics and advisory opinions
- Find more flexibility and work/life balance in the legal profession

The Lawyer's Essential Guide to Writing
By Marie Buckley

Product Code: 5110726 / LPM Price: $47.95 / Regular Price: $79.95

This is a readable, concrete guide to contemporary legal writing. Based on Marie Buckley's years of experience coaching lawyers, this book provides a systematic approach to all forms of written communication, from memoranda and briefs to e-mail and blogs. The book sets forth three principles for powerful writing and shows how to apply those principles to develop a clean and confident style.

Find Info Like a Pro, Volume 1: Mining the Internet's Publicly Available Resources for Investigative Research
By Carole A. Levitt and Mark E. Rosch

Product Code: 5110708 / LPM Price: $47.95 / Regular Price: $79.95

This complete hands-on guide shares the secrets, shortcuts, and realities of conducting investigative and background research using the sources of publicly available information available on the Internet. Written for legal professionals, this comprehensive desk book lists, categorizes, and describes hundreds of free and fee-based Internet sites. The resources and techniques in this book are useful for investigations; depositions; locating missing witnesses, clients, or heirs; and trial preparation, among other research challenges facing legal professionals. In addition, a CD-ROM is included, which features clickable links to all of the sites contained in the book.

How to Start and Build a Law Practice, Platinum Fifth Edition
By Jay G Foonberg

Product Code: 5110508 / LPM Price: $57.95 / Regular Price: $69.95

This classic ABA bestseller has been used by tens of thousands of lawyers as the comprehensive guide to planning, launching, and growing a successful practice. It's packed with over 600 pages of guidance on identifying the right location, finding clients, setting fees, managing your office, maintaining an ethical and responsible practice, maximizing available resources, upholding your standards, and much more. You'll find the information you need to successfully launch your practice, run it at maximum efficiency, and avoid potential pitfalls along the way. If you're committed to starting—and growing—your own practice, this one book will give you the expert advice you need to make it succeed for years to come.

Microsoft OneNote in One Hour for Lawyers
By Ben M. Schorr

Product Code: 5110731 / LPM Price: $19.95 / Regular Price: $34.95

Each copy of Microsoft® Office 2010 sold now includes OneNote, and its usage among lawyers is poised to skyrocket. With this guide, learn to use OneNote in your law practice to save time and increase productivity. Microsoft® OneNote in One Hour for Lawyers will explain, in plain English, how to get started with the software, develop best practices, and become far more effective in your note-taking and research. In just six, short lessons, you will learn how to:

- Get started with your first notebook
- Take notes more effectively
- Add audio and video recordings to notes
- Capture and organize side notes
- Collect research quickly and easily
- Create templates for frequently used notes
- Search and share notebooks
- Integrate OneNote with other applications such as Microsoft® Outlook and Microsoft® Word

Social Media for Lawyers: The Next Frontier
By Carolyn Elefant and Nicole Black

Product Code: 5110710 / LPM Price: $47.95 / Regular Price: $79.95

The world of legal marketing has changed with the rise of social media sites such as Linkedin, Twitter, and Facebook. Law firms are seeking their companies attention with tweets, videos, blog posts, pictures, and online content. Social media is fast and delivers news at record pace. This book provides you with a practical, goal-centric approach to using social media in your law practice that will enable you to identify social media platforms and tools that fit your practice and implement them easily, efficiently, and ethically.

30-DAY RISK-FREE ORDER FORM

ABA LAW PRACTICE MANAGEMENT SECTION
MARKETING • MANAGEMENT • TECHNOLOGY • FINANCE

Please print or type. To ship UPS, we must have your street address.
If you list a P.O. Box, we will ship by U.S. Mail.

Name _____

Member ID _____

Firm/Organization _____

Street Address _____

City/State/Zip _____

Area Code/Phone (In case we have a question about your order) _____

E-mail _____

Method of Payment:
❏ Check enclosed, payable to American Bar Association
❏ MasterCard   ❏ Visa   ❏ American Express

Card Number _____ Expiration Date _____

Signature Required _____

MAIL THIS FORM TO:
American Bar Association, Publication Orders
P.O. Box 10892, Chicago, IL 60610

ORDER BY PHONE:
24 hours a day, 7 days a week:
Call 1-800-285-2221 to place a credit card order.
We accept Visa, MasterCard, and American Express.

EMAIL ORDERS: orders@americanbar.org
FAX: 1-312-988-5568

VISIT OUR WEB SITE: www.ShopABA.org
Allow 7-10 days for regular UPS delivery. Need it
sooner? Ask about our overnight delivery options.
Call the ABA Service Center at 1-800-285-2221
for more information.

GUARANTEE:
If—for any reason—you are not satisfied with your
purchase, you may return it within 30 days of receipt for
a refund of the price of the book(s). No questions asked.

Thank You For Your Order.

Join the ABA Law Practice Management Section today and receive a substantial discount on Section publications!

Product Code:	Description:	Quantity:	Price:	Total Price:
				$
				$
				$
				$
				$
			Subtotal:	$
			*Tax:	$
			**Shipping/Handling:	$
			Yes, I am an ABA member and would like to join the Law Practice Management Section today! (Add $50.00)	$
			Total:	$

**Shipping/Handling:

$0.00 to $9.99	add $0.00
$10.00 to $49.99	add $5.95
$50.00 to $99.99	add $7.95
$100.00 to $199.99	add $9.95
$200.00 to $499.99	add $12.95

*Tax:
IL residents add 9.5%
DC residents add 6%